CROCHET FOR BEGINNERS

The simple guide to getting into the world of crochet. Learn how to crochet and create fantastic patterns through the step-by-step illustrations iincluded.

Second Edition

Tessa G. Ross

Mia Lee

TABLE OF CONTENTS

Introduction

If you are a beginner, a crochet pattern can certainly look like a foreign language. The first step in learning how to crochet is to learn the basics of crochet. When mastering a very basic crochet needle, there are a few easy-to-learn crochet needles like basketball points, popcorn points, and checkerboard prints! In this e-book, beginners follow one of the Afghan crochet patterns and make themselves a blanket, or give one to a friend. If you make your first Afghan, you can do another, another, and another! It is an addictive hobby. Crocheting an Afghan is a great gift for any occasion, including birthdays, weddings, baby showers, or just because!

So you've decided you are ready to learn how to crochet. You probably already understand you can't just read an article and learn all you need to know. But after reading this book, you will be able to get a good start in your pursuit of a crochet hook. Also, by the time you read the article, you'll learn where to find everything you need to know to crochet.

The first thing you need to know is what hooks are. The answers are quite simple. Crocheting is the process of making a fabric out of yarn using a crochet hook. To do this, you choose between an almost endless variety of ropes and yarns and many different types of supports. To make the fabric, you have loops of yarn or yarn of other loops. I know it probably sounds simple. The truth is that it is real. The key is that you need some skill and agility in your hands to do it right. You also need to have the right hooks, yarn, and instructions. You have to be careful you do things right, or you will end up with something you can't use instead of your own work of art.

An important aspect of crocheting is being successful in always choosing projects with clear written instructions. Once you have the correct written instructions, you just follow a guide that will make everything easier. When you have decent instructions, you will have the answer to many questions, such as what type of hook you need, what kind of yarn, what the right stitches are, and where to use them.

Too many people think they can only improvise instead of relying on clear instructions and just end up with a disaster. These people are frustrated and wish they had done things differently in the first place.

Knowing how important the instructions are, you will probably also see how important knowing the basic crochet terms are. Crochet instructions are usually written using shorthand and specific abbreviations. Examples are DC, which stands for double crochet, and SC, which stands for single crochet. You see, if you don't know it, you'll end up chasing your tail and wondering how you got yourself into this mess.

A common question beginners ask me is what the difference is actually between knitting and crocheting. There is a simple answer. When knitting, you use two hooks, and when you crochet, you only use one hook.

Chapter 1. The Easy Way to Understand and Start Crocheting

Before learning to read crochet patterns, here are some important guidelines you need to remember:

- Determine the crochet pattern you want to work with, and different patterns tell you which one will make a good scarf or a blanket. As a beginner, it is better to start with simple patterns first. The difficulty of the patterns is usually written under the title.

- Establish the size of the finished product. It is better to take note of what size the product should be, especially in garments where measurements of different parts vary.

- Are the materials complete? Buy the materials needed on the pattern you're going to work with. The type of yarn and the size of the crochet hook will be indicated on the pattern you choose.

- Make sample swatches to identify the size of your project.

- Know the stitches that will be used in making this pattern. They are most likely indicated at the beginning of the pattern, for example, single crochet, chain, half double crochet, slip stitch, and many more.

- Familiarize yourself with the keys and the abbreviations of techniques.

- When you encounter an asterisk, the pattern is telling you that the step must be repeated. Always begin with tying a slip knot onto your hook. Create a loop on the tip of the yarn, and then slide it onto the crochet hook. Enfold the yarn back over the hook, then again pull it through the loop, and lastly, pull the hook with one hand, so both ends of the yarn are being held to tie a slipknot.

- Start working step by step. The pattern will tell you how many chains you need to make. Steps are listed in order by the number of rows. Patterns always begin with a foundation chain that can be long or short.

- Observe the numbers of stitches at the end of the row; the number informs you of how many stitches you'll be working with. Try to count your stitches every 10 rows so you won't lose track of the pattern. You may also use an arrow counter, which can be an app, or just manually write down the current row you're working with on a piece of paper. There is also a row counter that can be attached to the hook so you can click every time you finish a row.

- Check if the pattern you are working on needs to be stitched together or blocked for the finishing step. Accessories like buttons and ribbons can also be added to the finishing touch.

When working on a crochet project, you need to follow a knitting pattern; and reading crochet patterns is like a code that must be deciphered. It may be an abbreviation or a term list, and as a beginner, you might get intimidated when you cross path with these alien terms, but worry not! Just invest a little effort, and soon enough, all these foreign abbreviations for you will be a piece of cake.

Once you've chosen the pattern you want to do a hands-on, read all the information and take note of all the important details such as the abbreviations used, the type of stitches, yarn and materials that are needed, gauge information and sizing and other pattern note that need to be jotted down.

Crochet terminology can be confusing for beginners when it comes to the dissimilarity between the US and UK abbreviations. Choose a pattern that is written in your language preference so you can get the right abbreviations. Also, consider that pattern keys can be somewhat written in different ways, such as the term "3ch," which means to make 3chains can also be written as ch3. When you get to be comfortable with the abbreviations, it will be easier for you to follow them given the slight changes.

Reading a crochet pattern is like learning a foreign language. It's quite tricky, and when you learn the abbreviations of crochet terms below, you may now start a basic pattern.

Crochet Terminology

- **Acrylic** –Synthetic yarn.

- **Back Loops** –The loops on the top of your crocheting work are the front loops. The ones behind these are the back loops.

- **Back Loops Only** - This means to focus only on the back loops.

- **Back Loop Single Crochet** - A variation of the single crochet stitch which focuses only on the back loops.

- **Coned Yarn** - Yarn that has been wound onto a cone-shaped holder.

- **Color Flashing**- This is an effect that can happen when using variegated yarn. It's when an unintentional pattern occurs, i.e., zigzags.

- **Double Crochet** - This stitch is taller than a single crochet stitch, and it's formed by the 'Yarn Over' technique.

- **Floats**- This describes the unused strands of yarn that are carried across the back of the project.

- **Freeform Crochet**- This allows the crocheter to explore the craft in unique and unexpected ways.

- **Frog**- 'To frog' = to rip out stitches. 'Frogging' = adding functional or decorative pieces, such as buttons.

- **Granny Square**- This is a crocheted motif made from a ring of chain stitches built outwards.

- **Half Double Crochet** - These are half a double crochet stitch.

- **Inelastic**- This is the yarn that is slow to recover its shape (or doesn't at all) once it has been stretched.

- **Kitchen Cotton** - This is a yarn that is useful for doing projects for kitchen use; potholders, dishcloths, placemats, etc.

- **Loops** - Loops are an integral part of crocheting and are created using the hook.

- **Pjoning** - This is using the slip stitch to create beautiful fabrics.

- **Place Maker** - Make a mark on your work (preferably one that can easily be removed) to help you locate a spot later.

- **Plarn**- 'Plastic Yarn'-often plastic bags that have been cut up and repurposed into yarn.

- **Scrapghan** - An afghan created from yarn scraps.

- **Shell Stitch** - Works multiple stitches into one single stitch.

- **Self-Striping Yarn**- A type of variegated yarn that has two or more colors. Often there are long lengths of each color before it changes.

- **Single Crochet** - A basic crochet stitch.

- **Slipstitch** - A loose stitch joining layers of fabric that isn't visible externally.

- **Tapestry Needle** - A hand sewing needle that's useful for adding embroidery.

- **Turning Chain** - A group of stitches that facilitates the transition between the rows of crochet stitches.

- **Treble Crochet** - A taller stitch than the double crochet.

- **Variegated Yarn** - Yarn that has more than one color.

- **Work Even** - Continuing in the same stitch pattern, without increasing or decreasing.

- **Worsted Weight Yarn** - A medium weight yarn.

- **Yarn Cake** - A method for winding yarn.

- **Yarn Over** - This is a stitch that involves wrapping the yarn from back to front before placing the hook in the stitch.

Common Crochet Terminology and Abbreviation

Terminology	Abbreviation
Chain	CH, ch
Single crochet	SC, sc
The half double Crochet	HDC, hdc
The double crochet	DC, dc
The treble crochet	TR, tr
The double treble Crochet	DTR, dtr
The extended single Crochet	EXSC, exsc
Cluster	CL, cl
Group	GP, gp
Right side	RS
Slip stitch	Sl st, SS, ss
Space	Sp
St(s)	Stitch(es)
Together	TOG, tog
Turning chain	Tch
Wrong side	WS
Yarn over hook	Yoh

When making a chain, you start with making a slip knot on the hook. The second step will be pulling the yarn over from the back and snatching it with a hook. Then drag the hooked yarn using a slip knot onto the crochet hook, and this step will make a single chain stitch.

Common Crochet Instruction Meaning:

- **Sk**-skip a stitch
- **Inc**-increase; make two stitches in the same space
- **Dec**-decrease; make two stitches combined together
- **RS**- right side
- **WS** – wrong side
- **Yoh**-yarn over hook
- **Beg**- beginning
- **Blo**-back looks only; working with your hooks only through the back loops
- **Flo**-front loops only; working you're your hooks only through the front loops.
- **Alt**-alternate
- **Approx**-approximate
- **Bet**-between
- **Bo**-bobble
- **BP**-back post
- **BPdc**-back post double crochet
- **CC**-contrasting colors
- **CL**-cluster
- **Cont**-continue
- **dc2Tog**-double crochet 2 stitches together
- **edc-**extended double crochet
- **esc**- extended single crochet
- **foll**-following
- **FP**-front post
- **Lp**-loop

- **M**-marker

- **MC**-main color

- **pat/patt**-pattern

- **prev**-previous

- **rem**-remaining

- **rep**-repeat

- **rnd**-round

- **sk**-skip

- **tch**-turning chain

- **tog**-together

- **yoh**-yarn over hook

- ***** repeat the pattern

- *** *** repeat the pattern between asterisks.

- **{} [] ()** -work with the pattern inside the bracket/parentheses

You can now practice your skills in reading pattern abbreviations with these sample pattern instructions.
Row 1:cH10; sc in 3rd ch from hook and in each ch across.

It means you'll make 10 chains first, and after that, you'll start working with a single crochet stitch on the 3rd chain. Remember to skip count the loop on the hook when counting the chains you made from the single crochet.
Now, let's try a double crochet.

Row1: cH20; dc in the 6th ch from hook and inch across 19 dc by starting with a slip knot on the hook, you'll now create 20 chains, and on the 6th chain from the hook you'll do a double crochet stitch to the remaining 14 chains, plus the 5 stitches that you skip will give you 19 double crochet stitches.

Chapter2.The Best Crocheting Tools and Materials

Crochet for beginners ought to be among the amazing hobbies one can have, and getting to know the material being used is fun. There are lots of impacts of crochet, and whether it is for financial or social use, the materials used are worth knowing one after the other. Seven basic materials are needed for any beginner to make beautiful crochet and another four materials that can help spice it up.

Here are the basic materials for starting up a crochet project:

- Yarn

- Crochet hook

- Scissors

- Darning needle

- Tape measure

- Hook organizer

- Stitch markers

- Row counter

- Stitch patterns

- Crochet book

- Crochet material organizer

The materials help in one way or another in making crochet. However, for beginners, one can use the basic ones.

Crochet Book

This is a tutorial book that helps a beginner to know hundreds of designs, both fancy and basic, and also easy to use. As the name suggests, it is a book that outlines pictorial information and insights on a couple of designs that have been elaborated. The book is essential for a beginner who intends to perfect the art by learning page per page and hook by hook. The book can be found online, and one can order it to be delivered to your country.

With the age of the Internet, if you cannot get the hardcopy, there are many tutorials on the Internet of the same type, and you can learn from various tutorials that can help you develop the art of crocheting. When you finally get to learn some designs, you can create your patterns and be creative too. Some of the professionals all over the globe started with a few designs and created others over the years, which have been adopted by the crocheting community worldwide. This means there is room for being creative and innovative.

Yarn

Yarn is a thread used in sewing or knitting any form of material. This is the backbone of crochet. It is the only material that comes out of the final product as it carries everything from designing to the conclusion. For beginners, it is advised to use a medium weight yarn as it is easy to crawl it with the hooks.

There are different types of yarns according to your preference, and it is better to understand them before buying them. The most common materials are polyester and wool. Nylon, acrylic, rayon, and viscose can also be the best choice according to one's preference.

Here are the types of yarns:

- Natural fibers

- Synthetic fibers

- Eco-friendly fibers

Natural Fibers

These are yarns made from natural materials.

Cotton

This is a material harvested from cotton plants; a process is used to preserve them to last longer

Silk

This is a form of material made from the larvae of silkworm and is mostly incorporated with other fibers to create a neat and long-lasting yarn.

Cashmere

Just from its name, you can see it is drawn from a cashmere goat and is known for being soft and warm at the same time.

Linen

This is harvested from a flash plant and is commonly used for light garments.

Wool

This is so common in clothes and yarn, and it is a perfect material for heavy yarns.

Synthetic Fibers

As stated above, one of the commonly preferred materials for yarn and are among the selling materials in the world. This includes; nylon, polyester, acrylic, rayon, and viscose.

Eco-Friendly Fibers

Organic Cotton

This is cotton made from cotton plants and is not treated with chemicals.

Bamboo

Bamboo has always created many products for different uses, and its silk is harvested as it makes a perfect yarn because of its strength.

Those are just a sample of the commonly used yarns which are formed from different fibers for different types of crochets according to users' needs.

Hooks

This is primarily the needles used to hook up and do stitching on yarn to form crochet. The hook drives the yarn on each one in a back and forth manner to form beautiful crochet. Sometimes, it is used concurrently with needles when a misstep is made on crochet.

Hooks come in different sizes, and it is better to choose a perfect one depending on the yarns' sizes and design. It is advisable to always consider all these before starting up, for some hooks may not perfectly fit your desired project.

Scissors

This is a tool commonly used in homesteads for homemade clothes or trimming of oversized curtains and towels. It is also known for being used by tailors for cutting their materials and another trimming of textiles. Scissors on crochet are also paramount.

Just like the hooks, the scissors have their types and different functions on a craft or any material using yarn and hooks. The basic one is the general craft scissors, which can be found locally and easily. It is okay to use the general craft scissors on different fibers because it does not leave sharp edges and cuts in a zigzag manner, just like the pinking shears. Here, the type of scissor does matter when the crochet is in the completion stage as it helps cut it into nice pieces without producing threads and tears in appropriately. When buying them online, make sure you check their specifications, as others might not be suitable for your project. There commended scissors are; standard, snips, embroidery scissors, and lastly, the dressmaker. Embroidery scissors could be perfect for this case because it helps cut the exact yarn used without tampering with the rest of the project.

Darning Needle

As the name suggests, it is a form of a needle with a bigger hole than the normal needle where the yarn passes through. The sharp end is a little blunt compared to a sewing needle and helps in making a perfect end on crochet. The darning needle is used to fix the end of each crochet to enable it to stay stable when in use. This is similar to sewing, where you tie a knot at the end of the material, but for crochet, the darning needle is used to make the knot, which will keep the whole crochet intact and in perfect shape.

There is no big problem when choosing a darning needle as one can compare the size of the yarn and its hole to see if it perfectly fits. The one with a larger hole can accommodate every kind of yarn, and there should not be any problem what so ever.

Stitch Markers

These are clips used to mark areas of interest in crochet. There are different designs of crochets, and when you have a slightly complex craft, it is always advisable for one to have a stitch marker. For beginners, it is always complicated to make crochets with corners or even rounded by following the pattern. This means the stitch markers are perfect for making areas where it forms patterns unless one is a professional.

Stitch makers have crafted clips that help indicate or put marks on a design to help a beginner or a craftsman to have a perfect and uniformed crotchet.

Any size and type of stitch markers can be used on any piece and type of yarn, as it does not favor the material. The marker can be found in local stores, and most people prefer them depending on the sizes of their hands or how perfectly they can hold them.

Tape Measure

Some of you could be wondering why almost everything used by tailors is being used to craft crochet, and the answer is yes, it needs to be totally perfect. Tailors are always seen with tape measures, and, to make crochet, you might want to get one too, especially for a beginner. The tape measure is simply for measuring and making the right adjustments when following a designed pattern.

This is a necessary tool when there is clipping using stitch markers as it will help to create uniform patterns with minimal or no blundering.

However, for crochet flowers, this might not be necessary as they are very simple and can be modified easily. Still, it is advisable for big projects and to avoid disappointments at the end of it with different and unorganized sizes.

Tape measures also come in different sizes and types and other specifications depending on the country you are located in. For a clear understanding, make sure you get a tape measure that supports your form of measurements. For instance, America's measurement is different from Russia's and the United Kingdom. To make perfect measurements, beware of the measures placed as some may be misleading or have different calculations depending on their form.

Stitch Patterns

These are the format you are achieving at the end of your projects. There are many designs and patterns you can get from the crochet book. A crochet book contains hundreds of designs and tutorials which can help a beginner with styles and a specific niche. This can also be found in tutorials of some craft enthusiasts who have knitted samples of crochets and might be a good chance to get out of your comfort zone and learn some styles or even create some at the end of the day.

For a specific stitch pattern, one can learn their way through and come up with perfect crochet by just following the simple rules. Listed below are some of the common stitch patterns for beginners that can be useful for your first project.

Twist Headband

These are perfect headbands one can make in one day for beginners. The twist headband can be put on the head, and it is perfect for the ladies to help hold their hair just like a clip. Unlike Marvin, it only covers a quarter of the hair and is comfortable and perfect for the winter season. This can be a good project for beginners.

Marion's Cozy Mug Warmer

Crochets are not only for wearing but for beauty; it is a craft and can be used in many forms. As the name suggests, this is a cover for a mug and is good for cold seasons. This is a unique design and also simple for beginners who are looking forward to creating beautiful designs.

Snowflake Patterns

Nothing is as perfect as a snowflake, and its design is even mind-blowing. It may look like a tiny piece, but when done, it is perfect crochet that can be made with easy steps. They can be used to beautify the house or even create designs in clothes.

Jingle Bell Stocking

When you hear the word jingle bell, what rings in mind is not a bell but Christmas. Yes, the stockings are made using yarn, and it makes a good crochet for a beginners' project. They are made to look like the Christmas attire for Santa Claus and can be spiced up using red and white colors.

With these stitch patterns, one can create a lovely design for beauty purposes or even gifting a loved one. A beginner should always keep an eye on the prize, which is the ultimate pattern that will be a result of the design.

Hook Organizer

After making the first and second patterns, you get to know the stitch patterns and designs that can work for you as you continue to be creative and innovative. The hook organizer resembles a toolbox for a car that is always referred to as "Do It Yourself" and can work on your car anytime, anywhere. For the crochet, this is almost similar as it carries your essential materials for the work.

After finishing the work, the hook organizer helps keep all the materials used as it has pocket-like spaces for placing hooks, tape measure, darning needles, yarn, and other combinations of crochet tools. One can make any design that can hold the materials with ease and keep them organized. Instead of buying a tool box for such materials, make one to be among the projects, and you will be shocked at how you continue to perfect your craft.

Chapter 3: Knitting and Crochet Differences

The capability to devise an undertaking from start to finish and see it via the mathematical potential is helpful, even though not strictly important, for both craft techniques.

Both knitting and crochet offer many extremely good health benefits.

Principally, each knitter and crocheter needs to have the endurance necessary to maintain running, creating stitch after stitch after stitch, until a task is finished.

So, what is the difference between knitting and crocheting? Why wouldn't it be counted whether or not you do one or the other?

It would not always be remembered beyond a private choice of the route. Still, the folks who might are getting to know it and have a little interest in yarn crafting will want to discover the variations between the two crafts for better information on which one is probably perfect for them.

Here are some of the differences between each craft:

Elements

With regards to materials, knitters, and crocheters, start with comparable yet special stashes; you may discover most of the differences inside the equipment department.

From time to time, the two needles are related by using a wire, as in a circular knitting needle.

If pointy needles are a part of the method, then the crafter in question is knitting with the aid of their hands.

Hand knitters are the simplest subset of the full quantity of knitters. In addition to hand knitters, there are also loom knitters and device knitters.

There are numerous unique types of looms and machines that can be used for knitting; they range from the easy to the complex, from the small to the huge.

 A few small machines may be used to knit socks or diverse other small initiatives. There are larger machines that may be used to knit sweaters, clothes, or other similar projects. Then there are large circular machines, some of which would not even fit in the living room of a median home, that mass-produce knitted fabric for the fabric companies.

Knitting machines promote very well the production of knitted fabrics from very exceptional threads and yarns. As an instance, t-shirt material is normally knitted.

Due to the fact crochet must be accomplished by using your hands, and it's tedious to apply such first-rate threads for crochet products, it is rare to find crocheted cloth as light weight and "drapery" as knitted t-shirt cloth.

The hook may be small or huge, or any size in between. It will usually be made from steel, aluminium, bamboo, plastic, wood, or bone, but it is honestly a nice hook.

Crochet is usually completed with the aid of the hands through the tools. A crocheter's moves are so intricate that, to this point, no one has been able to create a tool that can copy them.

There may be something in the fashion industry. This is referred to as a crochet system, but it does not sincerely make the same stitches like the ones made in crochet.

They devise blanket stitches that mimic crochet; however, upon closer examination, it is simple to see that it isn't always without doubt crochet.

So, to recap, crochet has executed the usage of a single crochet hook and is usually finished by hand in place with a tool.

This, the use of a crochet hook as opposed to needles or a system is what makes the sizeable distinction between the two crafts. But there are differences in tool significances in other variations as well.

Yarn

There are numerous distinct styles of yarn, and they can all be used similarly in knitting as in crochet, even though a few fidgety yarns lend themselves better to one craft or the other.

Thread is normally reserved for tiny crochet needles; it is no longer something used an awful lot in knitting.

There is a long-standing rumor that crochet makes use of an appreciably greater amount of yarn than knitting; however, many human beings have tested this, and it remains debatable as to whether or no longer it's true.

Structural Differences in Material

There are crucial structural variations between crocheted fabric and knitted material. Each crochet and knitting has yarn loops that are controlled.

With (weft) knitting (the kind of knitting that's closest to crochet), the loops build on each other in a way that requires a few active loops to stay on the needles.

Every stitch relies on the help of the stitch beneath it; if a knitter drops a stitch, the complete column of stitches underneath it might unravel.

With conventional crochet, there usually are not many active loops at one time—commonly only one loop, or in all likelihood a few loops.

(There are exceptions to this in a few superior stitches and niches of the crochet along with broomstick lace).

Tasks

It's highly impossible to objectively speak on which technique is "better" for any given form of undertaking. The fact is, the "pleasant" approach for any given assignment comes right down to personal choice. Each of these needlework techniques is well worth mastering and understanding their usage.

One motive that this query is so not unusual is that the variations in strategies mentioned more often were lower back while yarns have been so extraordinary and limited.

That's no longer the case these days, although, due to the fact the variety of both materials and advanced crochet techniques make it possible to create all of the identical objects that can be made with knitting.

An awesome example is with socks. Socks were once something best that knitters made, but now there are plenty of crochet sock styles.

Which Is Easier?

Ask this question to ten different yarn crafters, and you'll get ten different responses.

Many humans agree that crochet is a more comfortable craft to study than simply using the dominant hand. But, considering the other hand is used to help feed the yarn in crochet, it is not this easy.

Many humans do certainly find crochet is easier to choose up. But just as many humans who have tried both crafts find it's less difficult to knit.

Knit-Like Crochet

Individuals who aren't acquainted with knitting or crochet typically don't know the difference between the two at a glance.

Folks that craft in one or both of these forms quickly understand the stitches from knitting and those that may be most effective in crochet.

However, the variations among the 2 are more and tougher to discover because of many strategies that permit crocheters to create knit-like fabric.

Tunisian crochet is the most famous of those. It's a higher form of crochet that uses multiple hooks hung on longer hooks (and occasionally even round double-ended hooks!) to create knit- like cloth.

The opportunities are limitless, whether or not you need to include crochet or knitting or each!

Chapter 4: The Unbelievable Benefits of Crochet

Many people crochet to pass time. If you are in this category, you should know that you are doing yourself a lot of good. Not only does the time you spend making several designs help you to reduce accumulated body stress and anxiety, but it also helps you to:

- **Feel fulfilled.** You get to give yourself a pat on the back when you are done with a particular project. Imagine creating something from just a hook and yarn?

- **Relieve depression.** Now, there is something creative and constructive that you are thinking about. You will have less or no time for destructive and depressive thoughts. It has been proved that doing something you like doing makes the brain secrete hormones such as dopamine and serotonin. Dopamine works like an anti-depressant, making you feel good.

- **Be happy.** Crochet works are beautiful when well-done. You'll be happy to be the brain

- **Behind.** a beautiful piece of artwork.

- **You might make some extra income from it.** Especially in times where people have to work two or three jobs to make ends meet, selling beautiful crochet pieces might be a source of income for the crocheter.

- **Slow down or prevent memory loss altogether.** Memory loss can be slowed down when one partakes in logical exercises, such as crochet.

Also, it helps you to develop fine motor skills. People who have arthritis might do well to consider picking up crocheting as a hobby. It will help to keep their fingers nimble. The craft of crocheting will make you more patient. There is no rushing in it, it can only be done with the hands, so it will help you learn that some things take time. Working on stitches over time will also help you have a sense of focus and pay attention to detail. Not paying attention to detail might lead to frogging.

The list is almost endless, actually, but let's focus more on the bone of contention — what do you need to crochet successfully?

Clothing can be made in different ways, and one of them is crochet. Some of the other methods include weaving, bonding, and the one closely related to crochet, knitting. Crochet has, however, evolved from the process of making just clothing to making other decorative stuff. This means that you might not want to make a crochet dress for your baby, but you can decorate her nursery with crochet stuff. And why not make her a crochet dress anyway? I can bet that it will surely look good on her.

Crotchet is an enjoyable way out of boredom. There is no need to be idle anymore as you can make something beautiful during your free moments. You can take a leave from work, and while you enjoy your favorite movies

19

on Zee World, hold a hook and yarn in your hands and make a cozy blanket.

A definition of what crochet is might be a great way to start. You should be able to define what you do, right? To an informed eye, knitted and crochet works are just the same thing. However, knitting isn't the same thing as crochet. They are two different things.

Crochet seems to take less time as compared to knitting. Taking a keen look at both, crochet stitches usually take the form of a knotted look while knits seem as if you arranged so many 'Vs' in a straight line.

That's ultimately your choice to make, though. Knitting and crochet are both yarn crafts and require some time to finish. But if you find out you are not very patient, and you don't like making mistakes, especially one that will take a longer time to correct, I surely will advise you to take up crochet and ditch knitting (or at least in the meantime).

If you like to express your creativity in your patterns and don't want to spend much money on supplies, you are better off with crochet (even with your fingers and some yarn, you are good to go!).

Yarns can be classified based on their raw materials. These could be natural products (plants and animal sources) or human-made (synthetic). Natural yarns could be alpaca, wool, cotton, bamboo, silk, cashmere, or linen. Synthetic yarns could be made from polyester, acrylic, or nylon fibers.

There is also a third category: blended yarn, which is made from a combination of natural and synthetic fibers. Let's talk about three of the types as they are fit for beginners in crochet.

Acrylic yarn: I guess this is the most common type of yarn. It is affordable and fairly easy to maintain and will still look good after a long period of use. It can be a great starting material for a blanket. The use of acrylic yarn is not limited to crochet; it can be used for other purposes, e.g., hair extensions.

Cotton: as a material, it is lightweight, and the same goes for cotton yarns. Baby clothes can be made from cotton yarns as well as other intended light-weighted crochet works.

Wool: This is rather bulky, so it can be great for cold weather. You can use it to crochet cardigans, hats, etc. Wool is also great for a beginner crocheter because of its size.

Please note that the instruction will most likely specify the yarn to use. In cases where it is not specified, you can follow the guidelines above.

However, if you are a beginner, you can use any yarn that you are okay with (brightly colored and bulky, though). Once you master it, you can switch learning to practice with other yarn types. This is because different crochet patterns require different yarn types.

Chapter 5: Understanding Patterns

Patterns today are written instructions, often wrought with abbreviations. Before, in the early days of crochet, patterns were the actual crocheted items of someone else. For example, a lady wanted to crochet a wrist band. A written pattern was not available. Instead, she had to get an actual wrist band and painstakingly count the stitches and copy them. Then came the scrapbooks. Fragments of crocheted work were sewn on pieces of paper and bound together like a scrapbook. Some had crocheted samples sewn onto larger fabrics, while some were simply kept in a box or bag. Crochet stitch samples were also made in long and narrow bands. In 1824, the earliest crochet pattern was printed. The patterns were for making purses from silver and gold threads.

Early crochet books from the 1800s were small. These may be small (4 inches by 6 inches), but they contain a treasure of crochet patterns for lace, bands, lace-like collars, insertions, caps (women's, men's and children's), purses, and men's slippers. It also contained patterns for white crochet, which were for undergarment trimmings, mats, edgings, and insertions. The book recommended materials such as cotton thread, hemp thread, spool yarn and linen thread. Colorwork was done in chenille, wool, and silk yarns, with the occasional silver and gold threads.

The problem with these early patterns was their inaccuracy. For example, the pattern is for an 8-point star but would turn out to have only 6 points. These crochet books required the reader to rely more on the illustrations as a better guide.

Today, crochet patterns are more systematic, accurate, and organized. However, to the uninitiated, looking at a crochet pattern is a lot like looking at letters and numbers with no idea what they mean. Look for the meanings of the abbreviations, which are often printed at the bottom of the pattern. You can research some of the unfamiliar abbreviations.

A crocheter needs to learn the abbreviations and the symbols used in a crochet pattern. Without this knowledge, there will be a very limited number of patterns a crocheter can work with, as most are written in the crochet language.

Here are a few things to remember when working with patterns:

- Patterns are either made in rounds or rows. The pattern will specify if using either or both. Patterns come with a difficulty rating. Crocheters should choose the level best suited to their abilities. That is, beginners should stick to the pattern suited for their level while they are still

- Familiarizing themselves with the terms and techniques. Move to higher difficulty levels after gaining enough experience and mastery of the required crochet skills.

- Always count the stitches made while working and then after reaching the end of the row or round.

- Always check the gauge, especially if the project has to turn out the exact size and shape as indicated in the pattern.

- Learning to read crochet patterns requires practice and experience. Be patient and don't get

- annoyed.

How to Read a Crochet Pattern?

Crochet patterns would often only list the abbreviations and the number of stitches required for each row or round. Some patterns would also use abbreviations for other instructions, such as when to turn or when to begin and end.

The simplest crochet pattern would look like this:

Row 1: Use a size E crochet hook, cH15, single crochet 2ND ch from hook, and for each ch, turn. (14 single crochet)

In a professional crochet pattern this will be written as:

Row 1: ch 15, sc in 2nd ch from hook, 1sc in each st across the row. (14 sc)

This can look more like a foreign language for beginners. This is still the simplest of crochet patterns. Translated, the line means:

Row1: With a crochet hook size E, make 15 chain stitches. Starting on the 2ND stitch from the hook, make a single crochet stitch across the chain stitches. Then make a turning stitch. By the end of the row, there should be 12 single crochet stitches done.

Circle Patterns

Circles are also common in crochet. It starts with a center ring, which is the foundation of all rounds, as the foundation chain is to working in rows. The center ring is created either by making a ring from chain stitches or from in single chain stitch. The first method creates a hole in the middle of the circle crochet work. The second method has an inconspicuous center.

Another advanced technique to make a circle is with the magic ring. In this method, wrapped yarn around your fingers and make stitches in it. Pull the yarn tightly. With this method, there will be no hole in the middle of the circle.

Working With a Hole as a Center Ring

This is the most common way of making a center ring. A row of chain stitches is created and then looped off to make a ring. The hole in the middle is determined by how many chain stitches were made at the beginning. It also determines how many stitches can be made through the center ring. Avoid making the chain stitch too long because the resulting ring would be too large and unsteady.

1. Ch6 (make 6 chain stitches).

2. Place the crochet hook into the 1ST chain stitch, the one farthest from the crochet hook, and next to the slip knot. This will now form a ring.

3. Do 1 yarn over.

4. Through the chain stitch and the loop resting on the crochet hook, pull the yarn. This completes the center ring with a hole visible in the middle.

5. Working with a hole for a center is easy because the stitches are made by going through the center hole instead of into the actual chain stitches of the ring.

6. From the finished center ring above, make cH1 as a turning chain to be used for the single crochet of the first row.

7. Place the crochet hook through the center ring.

8. Make 1 yo. Pull the wrapped yarn through the hole. (center ring).

9. Make another yo and pull it through the 2 loops resting in the crochet hook. This finishes with 1 single crochet (single crochet).

10. Continue making single crochet through the center hole until it can't fit anymore.

Working with the Chain Stitch

This is another way of working in rounds. This is used when the pattern calls for a very small or barely noticeable center hole. Generally, one starts with a slip knot and cH1, and then adds the number of chain stitches required for a turning chain. For example, make 1 chain stitch then another 3 if using double crochet because the turning chains for dc are 3 chain stitches.

1. Ch1.

2. If using dc, make ch 3.

3. Perform 1 yarn over and place the hook into the center of the 4th chain stitch from the hook. This is the 1st ch made and is located next to the slip knot.

4. Make 1 double crochet into this chain stitch. Continue making dc on the other chain stitches. For beginners, a crochet pattern might look like it's written in a completely different language, and in a way, it is. Designers and crocheters use a language of abbreviations and conventions that are standardized, making it easy for anyone who understands this language to follow a pattern. The following is a breakdown of the most common ways the information is relayed in a crochet pattern – and what it all means.

Materials

This usually includes the yarn, hook size, and any extra notions or items. Sometimes patterns include the brand names of yarn or other items, but sometimes they merely contain the type of item needed (Lion Brand, Fishermen's Wool, Yarn versus 100 percent, worsted weight yarn, for example).

Gauge

Gauge is a dreaded word to even experienced crocheters, but it doesn't have to be. Put simply; the gauge is the measurement of the number of crochet stitches and rows per inch of fabric. Why is this important? Because achieving the proper gauge ensures that the finished item will turn out the correct size. Ignore gauge, and what is supposed to be a cropped, snug cardigan might become a house dress.

A pattern will indicate gauge either over 1 inch or 4 inches of stitches. For example, a gauge section might read: '3 stitches and 4 rows over 1 inch in single crochet'. This means that if the crocheter works a fabric in single crochet, he or she should have 3 stitches and 4 rows in every inch when using the hook size.

Before beginning a project, the crocheter checks that they are getting gauges by crocheting at least a 4-inch by 4-inch swatch in the pattern stitch, then blocking it, then measuring it carefully. If the gauge matches that given, it's okay to start the project. If the gauge does not match, the crocheter needs to change either the hook size or the yarn until they get the proper gauge. This is necessary because small differences in gauge can equal big differences in a finished item: a row of 30 single crochet at 3 stitches per inch will be 10 inches long, whereas a row of 30 single crochet at 4 stitches per inch will only be 7.5 inches long – not an unimportant difference.

The crocheter should generally change the hook size before changing the yarn. If the gauge is smaller than that given (e.g., 2 stitches per inch instead of 3), the hook is too large. If the gauge is larger than that given (e.g., 4 stitches per inch instead of 3), the hook is too small. Row gauge is much more adaptable in crochet, but the crocheter should still aim to get the gauge right of both.

Note that with some projects, gauge is more important than with others. For items with a lot of shaping, including sweaters, mittens, socks, and hats, a gauge is critical. For items that are more 'one size fits all', a small difference in gauge might be okay – a scarf that is an inch wider than the design intended isn't necessarily the end of the world.

Abbreviations:

Many times, this includes instructions for working special stitches. If a crocheter doesn't understand some of the stitches used in the pattern, the abbreviations are a good place to look for help. Many abbreviations are standardized, so as crocheters gain practice reading patterns, they learn to immediately recognize single crochet for single crochet, dc for double crochet, mr for a magic ring and, soon.

Instructions:

The instructions are the meat of the pattern, the place where the designer tells the crocheter what to do to make the item. For the most part, designers are explicit – 'Chain 3, work 3 for turning chain, double crochet into the third chain from hook' – but a few common shortcuts are used as well, including:

Asterisks:

Asterisks are used to indicate repeats of patterns. A pattern might read: 'Chain 1, slip stitch into the second chain from hook, *3 single crochet, ch2, 3 single crochet*, repeat from *to* three times, chain1, turn'. The stitches within the asterisks are repeated three times in the sequence they're given after the first time they're worked. So, in total, the asterisk would be repeated four times.

Parentheses:

Parentheses are used to indicate repeats, often within asterisks. The crocheter might see: '...*3 single crochet, (ch2, single crochet) twice, 3 single crochet*, repeat from *to* three times. To work the directions inside the asterisks, the crocheter would work 3 single crochet, 2 chains, 1 single crochet, 2 chains, 1 single crochet, then 3 more single crochet. Then the crocheter would repeat the instructions inside the asterisks the number of times called for.

Many crochet patterns are also broken down into rows (for flat crochet) and rounds (for circular crochet). Pattern repeats are often made up of many rows or rounds, which the designer will indicate in the pattern. At the end of the pattern, the designer will include any special finishing instructions, such as how to add embellishments or borders.

New crocheters should remember that although these are common conventions used in pattern writing, there are exceptions; designers are individuals, and some have their unique way of writing instructions.

Chapter 6: Different Types of Crochet

A variety of styles, patterns, and designs exist as far as crotchet works are concerned. Your style of crochet could be a factor of the instructions, your preference, and the result you have in mind, or the item you want to craft out. It is mostly a factor of the instructions.

We have added how to make some of these crochet types. You can only try them when you are done mastering the basics, though.

Bavarian Crochet

If you want to make a fancy shawl or blanket, you don't necessarily have to use the Aran style; you can consider the Bavarian as it might just be a perfect style of crochet for your project. Mind you, the Bavarian might take more time to achieve than the Aran, but trust me, the gain will be worth the pain.

Aran Crochet

Aran is a style of crochet with 'interlocking cables'. Consider this type of crochet when you want to make a blanket or a jacket, or you need some scarves or sweaters.

Amigurumi:

Remember those stuffed children's toys that you see made of crocheted yarn? That is Amigurumi. Amigurumi is a Japanese word which implies that the style originated from Japan. Amigurumi toys can also be knitted. Ami in Japan means 'knitted or crocheted' while Nuigurumi means 'stuffed doll.'

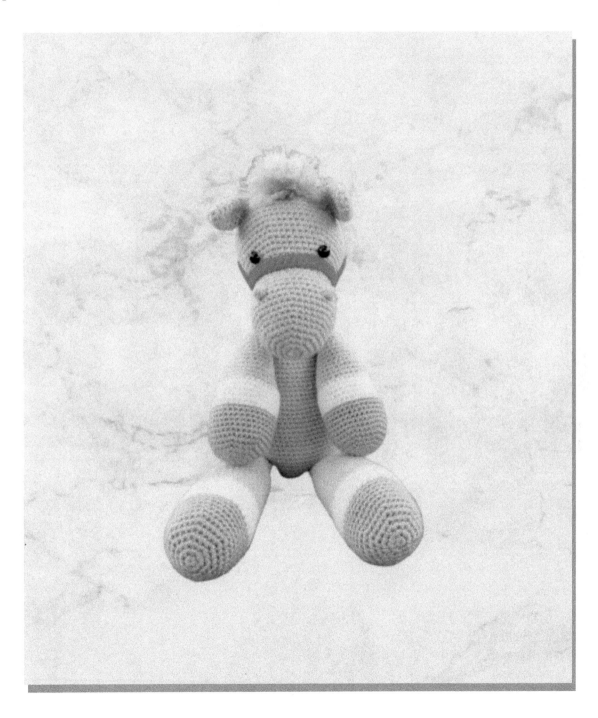

Bullion Crochet

Just as the name implies, it is a unique style of crochet that is designed for special functions, which is most often not clothing. It usually comes out as an evenly thick round crochet work. You can consider this style when you need a table mat or other pieces of decorative work.

Freestyle Crochet

You might just want to do it your way; with no measurements, no plan, no particular pattern for crochet work. You only need to conceive it in your mind and crochet-away. You can even add slight modifications as you progress, or you can decide to combine various styles most efficiently; that's why it is called a freestyle. Freestyle crochet will make a beautiful art piece if it is well done.

Chapter7: The Extra Layer Crochet

When an extra layer of stitches is added to an existing one, you have extra layer crochet. You can beautify a crochet piece or insert initials by using this style of crochet.

Filet Crochet

If you need open spaces in your crochet work, try using filet crochet. Filet crochet only uses two types of crochet stitches, and they are the chain stitch and double crochet stitch. Filet crochets are not worked from written instructions from graphs or symbol diagrams. Filet makes good decorative items such as table cloths and placemats.

Bruges Crochet

Your grand mum probably has one of these on top of her dining table, and you might have seen it on one of your visits. To make this style, you start with fine threads of stitches and then crochet them together to create beautiful lace patterns. Also, if you need an extra sparkle to your crochet design, think of embellishment with the Bruges crochet type.

Jiffy Lace Crochet

It is also called broomstick lace crochet. You will need two crochet hooks for this. A large one (or a material with a similar shape) and another one that might be smaller (depending on your preference). The second hook is used to form stitches around the large one. It is a high-quality crochet work that will always result in a beautiful piece if it is well done. You can consider this style when you need decoration items. A jiffy lace crochet will also look good on the upholstered arm of chairs.

Hairpin Lace

You will need three hooks for this design. Okay, don't get confused. Only one hook is required to work the stitches. However, the piece needs to be held between two hooks while doing the work. You can substitute any object with the same shape and size for the two hooks. You can use knitting pins or, better still, a hairpin loom.

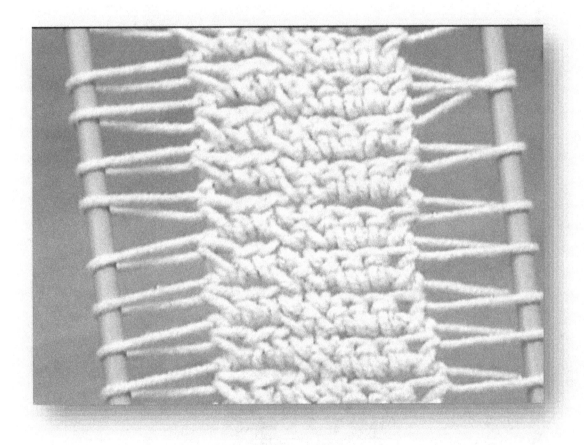

The hairpin lace must have gotten its name from the materials that were used for it initially; metal hairpins.

Bosnian Crochet

This is an old-style of crochet. It started in Bosnia, hence the name. Bosnian stitches are for patient folks because they are time-consuming and not advisable for big items. Most times, it is used in combination with other types or to close different types of crochet. When it is done, it looks like knitted work.

Tiny or Micro Crochet

The tiny crochet takes time as well. Well, if you have it, get a fine roll of thread and a smooth and tiny hook and get to work, as you can use this method to make dolls and jewelry. The tiny form in which they come out makes them very amazing.

Chapter8: The Shepherd's Knitting

It is also called the Afghan stitch or the Tunis crochet. It has a large number of stitches, so it is better to use long hooks.

Doily Crochet

According to the English dictionary, doilies are small ornamental pieces of lace or linen or paper used to protect a surface from scratches by hard objects such as vases and bowls; or to decorate a plate of food.
Doilies are usually made from fine crochet thread.

How to Make a Doily

As we have said before, doilies are better made from a thin thread, but if you're a beginner, you can use a double knit yarn. Your work will end up being bulkier than a regular doily, but you must have learned how to do it. Doilies are not for beginner crocheters, but you can always come back and give this a try after practicing the basic stitches over and over again. Here are the steps:

1. Start with making 10 chains.

2. Without removing the hook, insert it into the first chain and yarn over. (Both ends of the chain should be joined to make a circular shape)

3. Here's how you go about the next row/round:

4. Insert a stitch marker at the beginning of the row and chain 3 (make three chain stitches) counts these stitches as 1 double crochet.

5. On the base (foundation) chain, you need to insert your hook in the middle of the ring. Don't make stitches in the chains.

6. Make 23 double crochet in the ring. 24 double crochet in total including ch2.

7. Finish that row by making a slip stitch in the top chain of 1st double crochet.

8. Now make ch 4, count it as 1 double crochet and 1 chain.

9. Skip 1st st and make 1 double crochet and 1 chain in each stitch of the previous row. Total 24 double crochet.

10. Slip stitch to join this round.

11. This pattern is so easy and beginner-friendly, you can make it in no time.

12. Make 1 single crochet in ch1 space, make 3 chains, and 1 more single crochet in next chain 1 space. Repeat it till the last of this round. Slip stitch in 1st sc of this round to join this round.

13. Make 1 chain (don't count as stitch). 1 single crochet in chain 3 space, make 4 chains and 1 more single crochet in next chain 3 space. Repeat making 4 chains and 1 single crochet till the end of this round. Slip stitch in 1st single crochet.

14. Make 2 chains (don't count as stitch). 1 single crochet in chain 4 space, make 5 chains and 1 more single crochet in next chain 4 space. Repeat making 5 chains and 1 single crochet till the end of this round. Slip stitch in 1st single crochet.

15. Make 3 chains (don't count as stitch). 1 single crochet in chain 5 space, make 6 chains and 1 more single crochet in next chain 5 space. Repeat making 6 chains and 1 single crochet till the end of this round. Slip stitch in 1st single crochet.

16. Make 4 chains (don't count as stitch). 1 single crochet in chain 6 space, make 7 chains and 1 more single crochet in next chain 6 space. Repeat making 7 chains and 1 single crochet till the end of this round. Slip stitch in 1st single crochet.

17. If you want a bigger doily continue repeating this sequence.

18. Ch 3 (count as 1 double crochet) 6 more double crochet in chain 7 space.

19. 1 single crochet in next chain 7 space.

20. Continue repeating 7 double crochet in chain 7 and 1 single crochet I next ch 7 space. Slip stitch in 1st stitch.

21. Finish it off by leaving a tail of about 7 inches and cutting the yarn. Weave the tail into the crochet piece with a darning needle.

22. Your doily might not hold its shape, so you should put it entirely in water.

23. Bring it out and squeeze out excess water till it is damp. Fix it firmly by spreading it out on a piece of paper and sew the doily to the paper.

24. Ensure the paper is air-dried by hanging it.

25. Detach the doily from the paper when it is dry. The doily should hold its shape when it's dry.

Finger Crochet

When you drop your hook, and you deftly maneuver the yarn into a beautiful crochet work, you have finger crochet. You can use your fingers from start to finish, or you can finish it up with a hook.

How to Make a Finger Crochet Scarf

Finger crochets are best made with thick yarns. It is good to note that finger crochets are made the same way just as normal crochets. The only difference is that in this case, you have to use your fingers instead of a hook.

Bulky Yarn for Finger Crochet

So far, we have only been talking about using a single piece of yarn at once for your crochet projects. However, for finger crochets, you can use2-3 strands of yarn simultaneously to get a bulkier crochet piece. A crocheted piece with alternating colors can be made this way. But since the focus is on beginners, let us keep it simple by starting with just one strand for a simple scarf or shawl (a rectangle) and working double crochet stitches.

You start by making a base chain. Like we have said before, it is just the same steps as making double crochet. Let's go over it again because no hook is involved this time.

Step1: As in the image below, create a slip knot around your index finger.

Step2: Make chain stitches. Do this for the required length of the base chain. (How long or wide you want your scarf to be).

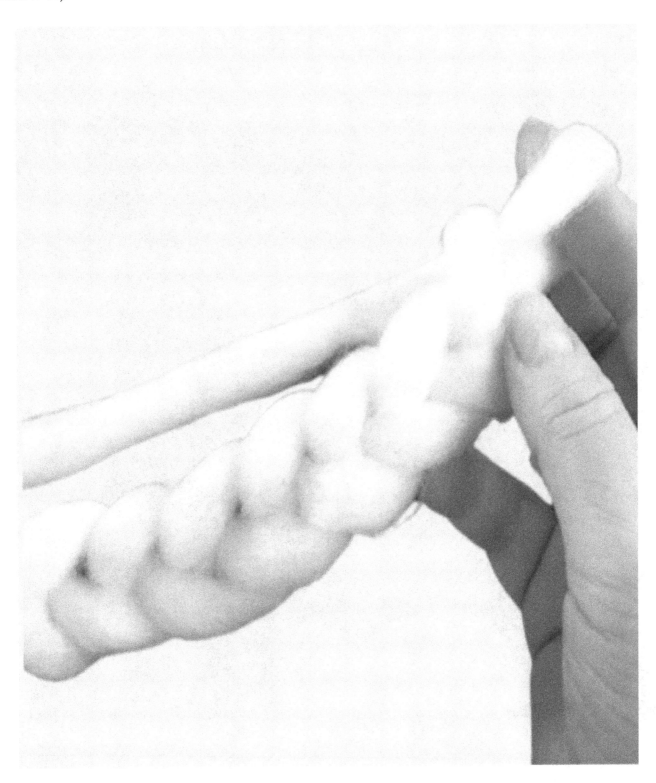

Step 3 (single crochet): While your index finger is still inserted in the last loop, inject the same finger into the third chain from your finger.

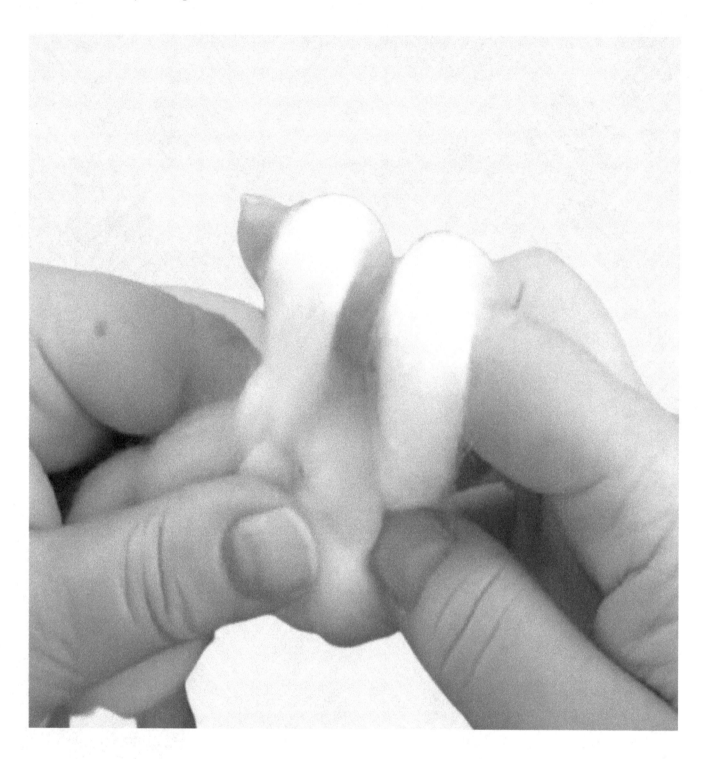

Step 4: Draw up yarn through the loop. Two loops should be on your finger as of right now.

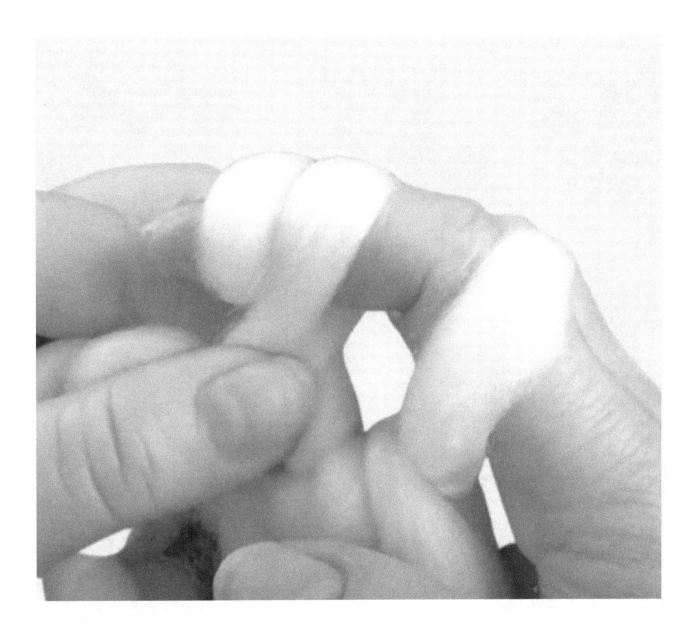

Step 5: Repeat the yarn over again, and this time, drag the yarn through the two loops on your finger to create your first Single crochet stitch. Make a complete row of single crochet stitches.

Step 6: To make a double crochet stitches, make 2 chains in beginning of the row. Yarn over and insert finger in chain, draw a loop from hook.

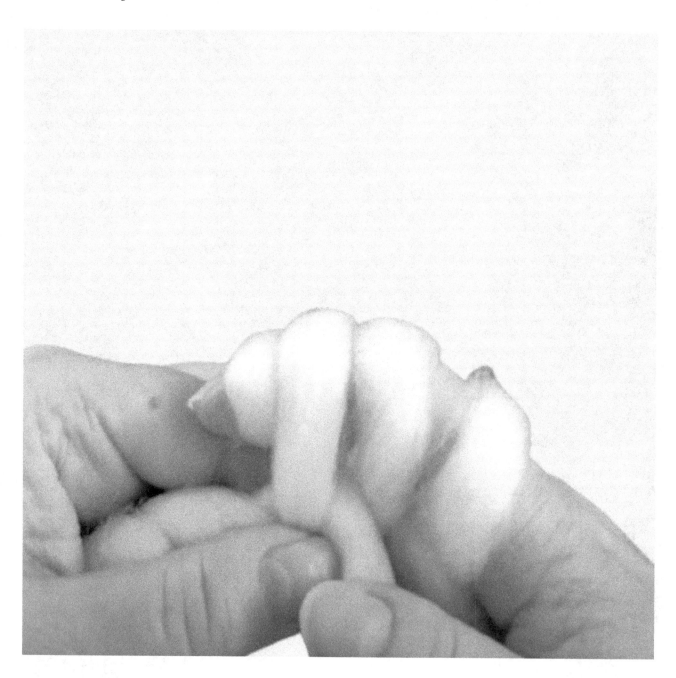

Step 7: Total 3 loops on your finger. Repeat yarn over, draw a loop from 2 loops. Yarn over again and draw loop from 2 loops on your finger. Now it's your first double crochet stich. Reapet a full row of double crochet stitches

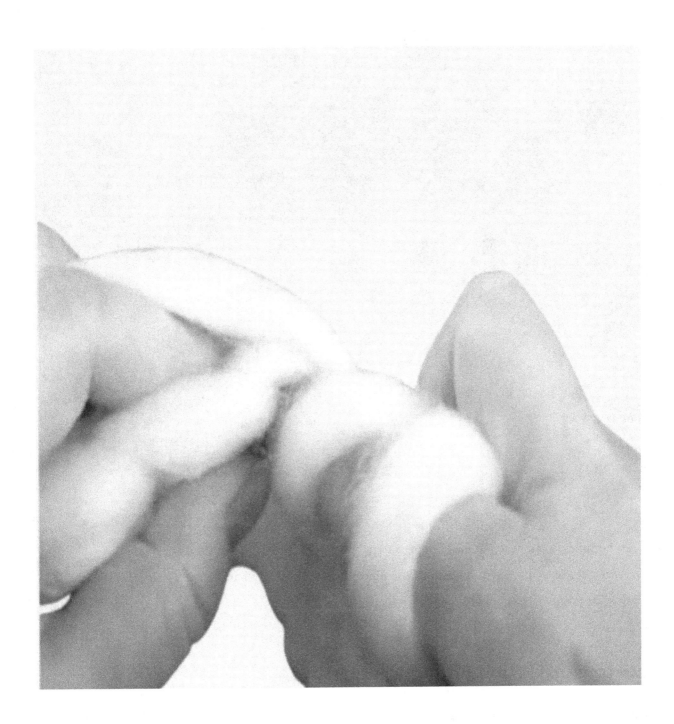

Step 8: Work more crochet stitches until you are done with the row.

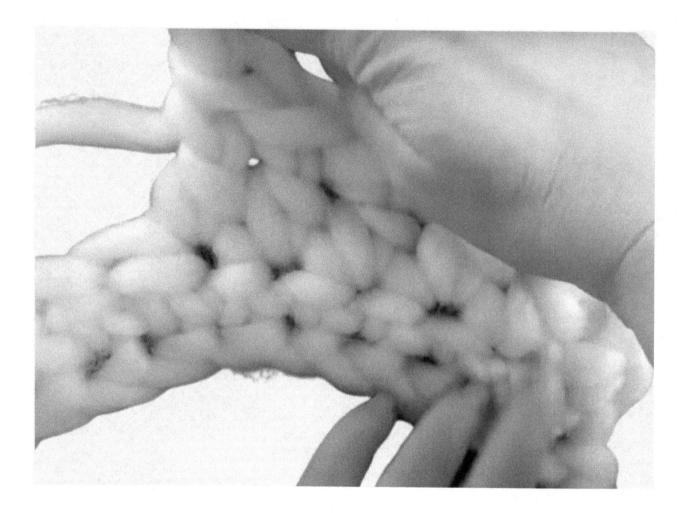

Step 9: To complete your scarf or shawl, repeat steps 7-8 to complete your desired scarf length.

Step 10: Allow at least 7 inches to the end of the piece to serve as the tail and cut off the yarn. Pull the tail through the last loop and deftly make a knot to secure your shawl.

Your scarf or shawl is ready for use!

Points to Note When Finger Crocheting

Stick with short stitches; your finger can only take a certain amount of loops at the same time. Working tall stitches are not the best for finger stitches.

Try to keep your work loose. Don't tighten your loops and chains too much.

Clothesline Crochet

This style is a darling when it comes to making baskets and some other round objects. You start it by making thick stitches as a kind of base or frame, and then you start to make more stitches while ensuring a round shape

You probably noticed there is an emphasis on 'doing it well.' Crochet works are beautiful when well done. That is why we wrote this book; to help you to do it well.

With this knowledge, I am sure you can't wait to learn how to make your first crochet stitch. So, get your materials ready, and...

Keep reading to learn more.

Chapter 9: Secrets Crochet Tips and Tricks Just for You

Here are some useful and helpful tips and tricks that will make crocheting simpler and keep you increasingly sorted out.

1. At the point when the afghan you're crocheting turns out to be excessively long and substantial, place stitching rings around the end you've just wrapped up. It will make it simple to flip it over when crocheting the following line only.

2. At the point when somebody approaches you to do something for them, write it down on a notepad. Write their name, when they require it by, and the thing they need to crochet. Additionally, record where the pattern can be found. At the point when you finish the crocheted job, snap a photo of it and keep it in a photograph collection, so when somebody asks what you crochet, you can show them.

3. Stringing a huge looked at needle with the free strings after completing a venture and meshing the loose lines into the undertaking is more straightforward than utilizing the hook. It just takes minutes to do an entire cover with numerous string changes.

4. If you are a beginner and regularly lose your place, write down the patterns on lined paper, each guidance in turn.

5. When traveling, utilize an empty plastic coke bottle to prevent the hooks from getting away.

6. To keep squares perfect as you crochet them before assembling them, keep them in a secured plastic pack. Utilize a little cushion of paper and pen to monitor what number of squares you've made.

7. Utilize a little self-clasping pin to hold a stitch when you set a project away.

8. The fabric store sells yarn cutters to wear around your neck. Keeping cutters on a yarn around your neck will prevent you from continually looking for them. The fabric store sells them.

9. Prevent skeins and balls from getting tangled by cutting a gap in the highest point of an unfilled plastic espresso holder, at that point softening the edges of the opening with a lighter or match to prevent the fleece from catching. If you have a few activities going on simultaneously, use marks or tape on the tops or sides of every compartment to write the task name and other significant data. Tape a little piece of dryer sheet inside every head to keep the fleece smelling pleasant and forestall static.

10. Utilize a three-ring fastener with clear sheet binders to arrange your patterns. Utilize a pencil pocket likewise with three gaps for additional hooks, measure check, and whatever else you need to keep convenient.

11. At the point when you open another crochet ball of string, take the paper and put it inside the focal point of the ball. At that point, when you need a new series, you'll have the shading and all the data for your next ball of string.

12. Utilize a toothbrush holder to hold your hooks.

13. It's anything but difficult to find, and you can drop hooks in your handbag and go.

14. To store scrap yarn, purchase a reasonable collapsible hamper, put a similar shading yarn in plastic essential food item packs, and save every one of the sacks in the hamper.

15. Take a two-liter plastic jug and slice the center to make an entryway. At that point, place your huge yarn inside and put the string through the neck. It keeps the 8oz yarn sorted out.

16. Make your new hook smooth by rubbing it into your hair.

17. To keep woven-in ends from coming free, weave on an oblique line rather than straight up or over.

18. To keep your crochet yarn/cotton ball from moving over the floor, put it in a little plastic storage bag with handles, drape it on your arm, and crochet in comfort.

19. Utilize a bobby pin as a marker for the finish of rounds. It comes off and on effectively and doesn't shred like piece yarn markers. You can likewise utilize bobby pins to hold the last stitch if you have to take the work free.

20. Store yarn in a zippered sofa-bed sack.

21. Paperclips make extraordinary stitch counters. Simply pop one on the stitch you need to stamp. Safety pins work incredibly as well and are somewhat simpler to put on and take off.

22. Utilize a wooden wine rack for yarn stockpiling. It works extraordinary, looks dynamite, and is a pleasant conversation piece.

23. Empty medicine bottles can be convenient for keeping smaller crochet instruments like column counters, dabs, and yarn needles.

Since you're composed, have a ton of fun crocheting!

Top Crochet Hacks

Do you ever think about how others get their crochet activities to turn out so beautiful? While part of having a venture turn out well has to do with training, there are different tips you can use to improve your crochet aptitudes. Regardless of whether you are merely starting to figure out how to crochet or you have been grinding away for quite a long time, here are ten tips that you can begin utilizing today! Learn things like what yarns to use, how to wind yarn, making new stitches, and the sky is the limit from there.

1. Do you love to crochet yet you have little youngsters and think it's difficult to get enough time for your pastime? Why not get them included? They love it since they had the opportunity to invest energy with you and help mom too.

2. Avoid blending various kinds of yarn in a similar undertaking. Multiple yarns, for example, cotton and acrylics, will dry at different rates after they have been washed. The final product is that your crochet venture that had looked so lovely once it was finished will look misshaped and exhausted after it has been removed.

3. Are you searching for a simple method to twist yarn into the ideal ball each time? Essentially fold the thread over two fingers. At the point when you are done, pull your fingers out of the ball.

4. Use post-it-notes to monitor your advancement as you take a shot at a venture. As you complete each line, move the post-it-note to the following line with the goal that you will never lose your spot. Furthermore, you can make notes or monitor the number of repeats you have done legitimately on the post-it-note. When it turns out to be full, simply start utilizing another one. Also, if you find mistakes or make changes to the pattern, you can record them on the post-it-note and keep it on that spot for when you utilize the pattern again later on.

5. To keep a crochet venture looking perfect and clean, consistently mesh the last parts of yarn into your project as you chip away at it. One route is to utilize a yarn needle to weave the yarn in, making it exceptionally secure and more reluctant to unwind.

6. A simple approach to make new stitches is to embed your crochet hook under the two circles of the stitch on the past line. Like this, when you complete a stitch, you will consistently have a ring still on your hook, making it simpler to start the following stitch. When tallying what

7. Number of stitches you have finished in that column, never incorporate the stitch that is still on the hook.

8. To monitor exceptional stitches or the finish of a column on your crochet venture, you can utilize plastic split ring markers. If you don't have any, or if you come up short on them, you can generally utilize self-locking pins, scrap yarn in an alternate shading, or even twist ties. They all work a similar way, and you can set aside cash if you, as of now, have these things available.

9. Often patterns will give directions for a few distinct sizes on a similar line in the model by utilizing brackets. To monitor which size you are crocheting, basically feature or circle the size you have chosen before starting the design. Like this, you won't incidentally begin adhering to the directions for the wrong size.

10. Many individuals find the winter months dull because of the chilly climate and absence of daylight. To help cheer yourself up, work with splendid hues that are fun and enthusiastic. Also, ensure you put resources into a decent light that gives loads of view while you work.

11. If you are working with a pattern that changes hues frequently, for instance, while making a checkerboard impact, don't start and stop each shading each time it turns. Prop the shading up via conveying it over the past column and stitching over the yarn. At that point, when the pattern requires the shading change, the new shading is prepared and sitting tight for you to utilize. Additionally, with this technique, you don't need to weave in the last parts of the yarn.

Basic Crochet Tips

When you start crocheting and have aced the fundamental stitches, there are, in every case, little issues that crop up repressing your advancement and destroying the completion of your work. By following these crocheting tips, you will guarantee a neater and all the evener completion to your job every single time you crochet.

Tip 1: Insufficient Space When Working in the Round

Here and there, when working in the round, there doesn't appear as though there is sufficient space to use the entirety of the suitable stitches into the middle ring. If you have this issue, DO NOT work over the highest point of the recently worked stitches, instead of doing the accompanying:

1. Augment the keep going circle on your hook and expel the hook from your work.

2. Starting toward the start of the round, delicately push your stitches up together, making a space toward the finish of the round.

3. Re-embed your hook, fix the circle and keep crocheting.

4. Rehash this procedure until you have completed the round.

Tip 2: Unexpected Gaps in Your Work or Extended Stitches

Sometimes, you may find you have a couple of gaps in your crocheting that ought not to be there, or that a portion of the stitches appear to have extended as the following line is by all accounts pulling them. The purpose behind this is typically straightforward; you are not crocheting into the right part of the stitch in the past column. Redress this consistently guarantee after embedding your hook into the stitch on the line underneath that you have experienced the two circles of the stitch, except if the pattern discloses to you generally, as in loopy holey patterns.

Tip 3: Split Stitches

Should you notice a split stitch, don't simply leave it. This makes your work look unattractive as it puts little parts of stitches over the pattern, which are entirely recognizable and cheapens the original crochet pattern. The time it takes to redress these split stitches will be very much compensated for having the work look flawless and clean. Should you locate a split stitch, expel your hook from your crocheting, fix everything up to and including the split stitch, reinsert your hook and recommence crocheting once more. It truly merits the additional exertion!

Tip 4: Finding It Difficult to Crochet into the Established Push

The primary line of any crochet venture is consistently the hardest. It tends to be hard to crochet into a sequence of chain stitches, particularly if you are utilizing slight yarn and a little hook!

If you think it's challenging to crochet the first push, take as a tab at crocheting the establishment push with a hook one size larger than the one required for the pattern. This will make the chain establishment push somewhat looser and the stitches slightly bigger. This won't appear on the final product; however, it will help you when attempting to embed your typical hook into the right part of your many chain stitches.

Tip 5: Crocheting Starting to Twist

If you find that your work is starting to twist after working the first couple of lines when working the straight-line strategy, it is because of your strain. You have crocheted the establishment push more tightly than you have crocheted the remainder of the pattern. To comprehend this, you have two alternatives:

Utilize a hook one size more significant to crochet the establishment push than the hook required to crochet the pattern.

Utilize the equivalent estimated hook yet make your work (establishment push) much looser.

Tip 6: Trouble Seeing Where You Ought to Crochet

At the point when first figuring out how to crochet it very well may be hard to see precisely what part of the stitch you ought to crochet into, mainly if you utilize dull hued yarn. So when first figuring out how to crochet using light-hued threads and strings, which makes the stitches much more straightforward to see, progress onto darker hues as your insight and certainty develop.

Tip 7: Losing Stitches

Tallying your stitches is one of the essential tips for crocheting effectively. It is additionally one of the most widely recognized issues to find that after crocheting a column, you have fewer stitches than the pattern says you ought to have, or with which you started with if not following a crochet pattern. The most well-known misstep is to lose stitches toward the start and additional parts of the bargains. This is expected to precluding working in the first or last stitch of a column. So if you end up in this position, check your beginnings and parts of the bargains before taking a gander at the body of the line itself!

Tip 8: Rectangular Work Decreasing Inwards or Outwards

This issue follows from the one above and is because of either increasing or lessening stitches without acknowledging it! You should check your stitches consistently to guarantee you have not left any out or coincidentally added any. Again, losing or including stitches toward the start or end of articles of clothing is the most widely recognized blunder and ought to be checked before the body of the column.

Ideally, a portion of these tips will be valuable with your next crochet venture. Simply remembering these pointers next time you get your crochet hook will in itself help your crocheting to look progressively proficient and flawless.

Chapter 10: Techniques and Stitches

There are many more advanced techniques and stitches that can make your crocheting projects much more aesthetically pleasing and fun to create.

Techniques

Double Strands

Some patterns will instruct you to work with two strands of yarn at once; these can be two of the same color or two different. All you would need to do to achieve this is to use both strands to create your slip knot and then continue to treat both strands as one while you work.

Increases and Decreases

To increase – or inc – in crochet, you simply work in more than one stitch, as specified by the pattern, into the same hole. This will increase the number of stitches in the current row you're working on.

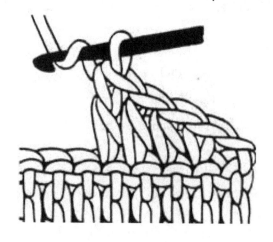

To decrease – or dec – you work in the first stitch as specified, skipping the final step of the stitch. This is the part where you draw a final loop through the loops on your hook, which leaves the worked loops on the crochet hook, before moving onto the next stitch. When you have completed the second stitch, you'll draw the yarn through all of the stitches on your hook to draw the first and second stitch together, leaving you with fewer stitches in the current row.

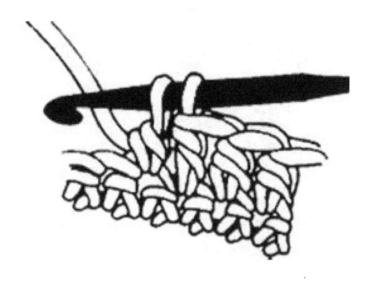

Changing Colors

Once you have started crocheting, there will be a point in which you'll want to change the color of the yarn you're using. To do this, you need to:

1. Start the work in color A.

2. When you're at the point that you wish to change, work as far as the last single stitch in the row or round, but leave the final stitch unfinished.

3. Grab color B with your crochet hook.

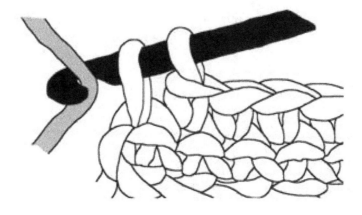

1. Pull up a loop with color B. You may need to gently tug the yarn of color A to keep the loops from getting too big.

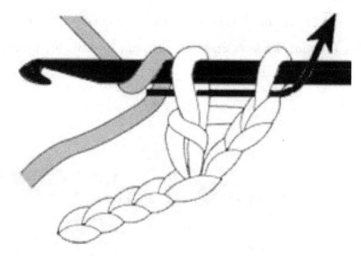

2. You then need to decide whether or not to cut color A. If you're going to use it again within the next few rows, it is better to leave it as it is, but if not, then you'll want to cut the yarn with approximately six inches to spare, which you'll weave in later.

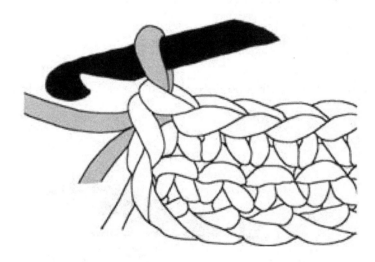

Working in the Round

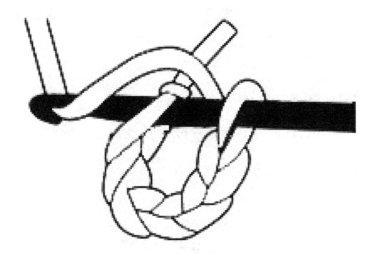

To begin a crochet pattern that works in rounds, you first need to create the center ring and crochet the first round. After completing the number of stitches required in the first round, join the first and last stitches to complete the circle. Here are the steps to do this:

1. Chain 1 stitch, making the turning chain for single crochet.

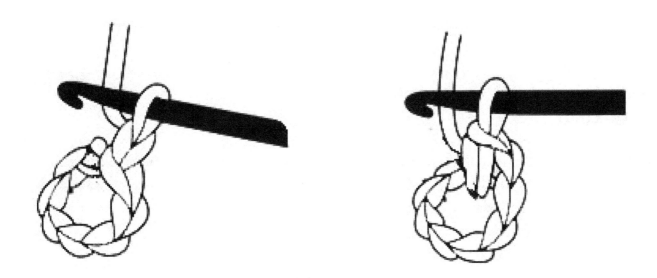

2. Chain 3 stitches to create the turning chain.

3. Work 1 double crochet stitch under the top 2 loops of the first stitch, the stitch directly below the turning chain. Remember, you do not need to turn your work.

4. Work 2 double crochet stitches into each stitch around, and then join the first and the last stitch of the round with a slip stitch, completing the round.

Making Cords

A cord has multiple purposes and is often thought of as something you knit, but as you can see from the direction below, you can also use crochet to create one.

1. Take two long lengths of yarn and double them over.

2. Make a slip knot on your crochet hook with both these pieces of yarn.

3. To make the first stitch of your cord, pull the first loop through the second.

4. To finish, pull one of the yarn pieces through the opposite loop. Pull the yarn tight and secure and tie two knots for each strand.

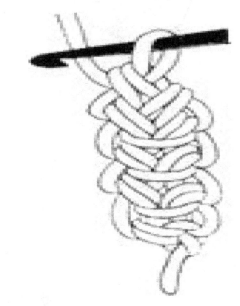

Joining Yarn

This is an important step in crocheting because if you reach the end of a ball of yarn but need to continue the project, you want this to be seamless not to spoil the appearance of your work. To do this, follow these steps:

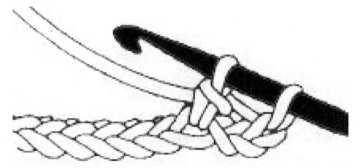

1. Double crochet across the row, stopping before the last stitch of the row.

2. Work the last double crochet stitch to the point where 2 loops are left on the hook.

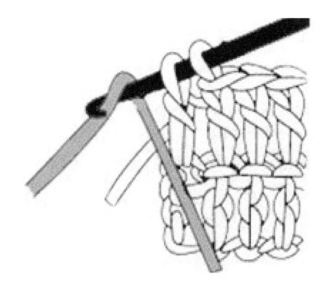

3. Draw the new yarn through the 2 loops on your hook.

4. Remove the loop from your hook.

5. Draw the tail end up through the stitch.

6. Stick your hook back through the hoop to begin your next row.

Sewing Together

A great way to join crocheted pieces together is by using a technique called the whip stitch.

1. Align the pieces you'd like to join together.

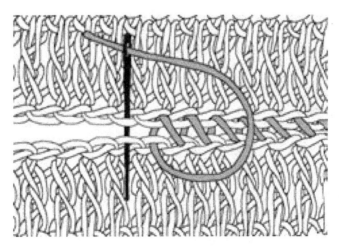

2. Draw the yarn up and over the 2 loops of the first stitch.

3. Repeat the last step through the entire edges to be joined.

Sewing on Buttons

There are many reasons you may wish to add buttons to a crocheted project. Whether it's for decoration or practicality, the way you administer them is the same:

1. Use a thread that matches your crocheted project.
2. With the backside of your project facing you, slip your needle through a few of the crocheted chains.
3. Pull the thread through until the tail is almost gone and wrap the thread around a single strand of yarn a few times to secure it.
4. Pull your needle through the project to the front in the position that you wish to attach your button.

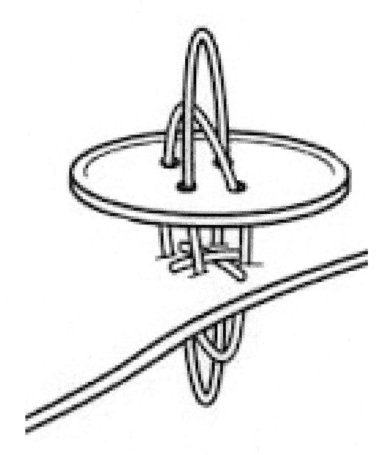

5. Sew the thread through the button and the project a few times to secure it.
6. Finish at the back of your project, repeating step 3 to secure the button.

Making Pom-Poms

Pom Poms are very simple to make and are a great addition to a crochet project. To create a pom-pom, follow the instructions below:

1. Continuously wrap the yarn around 3 of your fingers, approximately 100times.
2. Gently slide the bundle of yarn off of your hand.
3. With the same colored yarn, tie the bundle together in the middle.
4. Cut all of the loops on the yarn and trim the shape as desired.
5. You can then sew this to your project using a needle.
6. If you want to increase or decrease the size of the pom-pom, use a different number of fingers and wrap it around less or more times. Pom poms are very simple to create, and the more you make, the better you will get at making them.

Stitches

Making Ridges

Ridges can be crocheted for a number of reasons; to add detail to a design, to finish something off nicely, or even to give a textured effect. To do this, you need to:

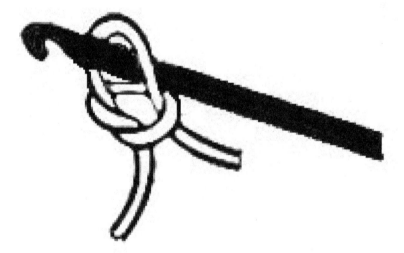

1. Make your Slip Knot stitch and create your foundation chain.

2. Start with a double crochet stitch and repeat this along the row.

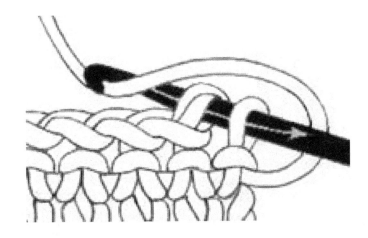

3. Create a slip stitch in the turning chain to end this row.

4. Chain 3 stitches and slip the first stitch to create a double crochet stitch in the back loop of the second stitch away from the hook.

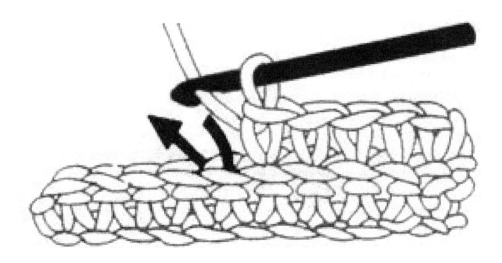

5. Repeat these steps until you have the ridge that you desire.

Shell Borders

Shell borders are very popular as they give a crochet project a pretty edge without being too fussy or difficult to do. To crochet a shell stitch:

1. Make a slip knot and crochet your foundation chain.
2. Work in a single crochet stitch into the second chain from your hook.

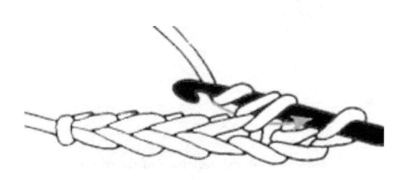 

Forming Picots

The picot stitch is usually used as edging and added onto a finished garment. You can either start along the edge of something you have already created or begin by creating a foundation chain of stitches.

1. Single crochet in the first stitch, then chain 3 stitches and single crochet in the next stitch.

2. Single crochet in the next 3stitches.

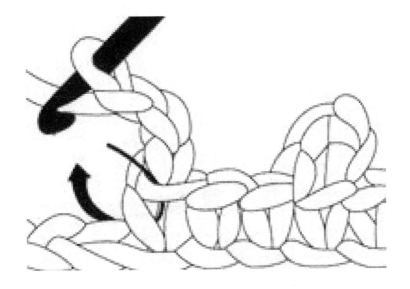

3. Chain 3 and single crochet in the next stitch – forming the picot.

4. Repeat steps 2 and 3 until you reach the end of your work to create a chain.

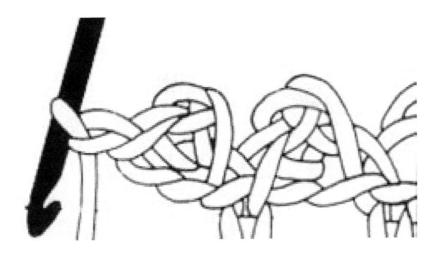

Making Different Shapes

The possibilities when crocheting are endless, and shapes are a good place to start as they are simple but very good practice for getting to grips with the basics. Below are the details for how to create some basic crochet shapes.

Circle

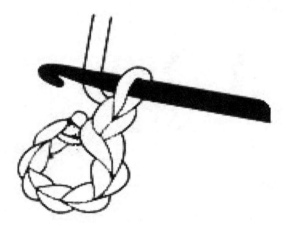

1. Start by working around.

2. Work 2 stitches into each stitch of the previous round.

3. Work 1 stitch into the next stitch, then 2 stitches into the next stitch all around, ending each round with a slip stitch.

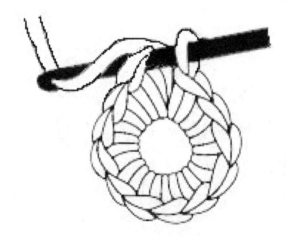

4. Repeat step 3 until the desired size is achieved.

Square

1. Make a slip knot and create your foundation chain.

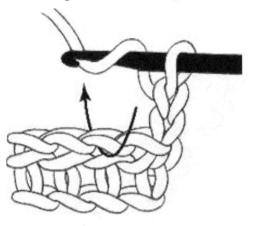 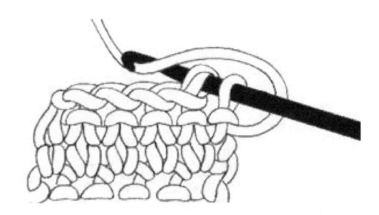

2. Create a half double crochet stitch.

3. Turn your work at the end of the row and repeat steps 2 and 3.

4. Repeat step 4 until the square is complete.

Triangle

1. Make a slip knot and create 1 chain stitch.

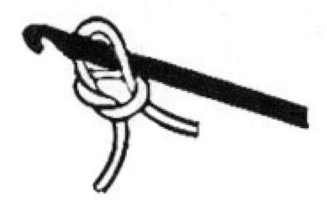

2. Turn your work and increase 1 stitch at the beginning and end of the row.

3. Repeat step 2 until the triangle is complete.

Crochet Flowers

A flower can be a great accessory added to a garment or household project. To crochet a flower, you need to:

1. Make a slip knot and create a foundation chain of 6 stitches.

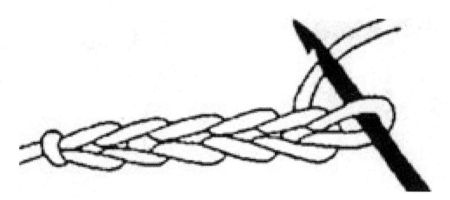

2. Use a slip stitch to tie up the ends of the chain, creating a circular shape. This counts as your first double crochet stitch and will be the base for the petals.

3. Make 14 double crochet stitches into the loop, forming the next ring

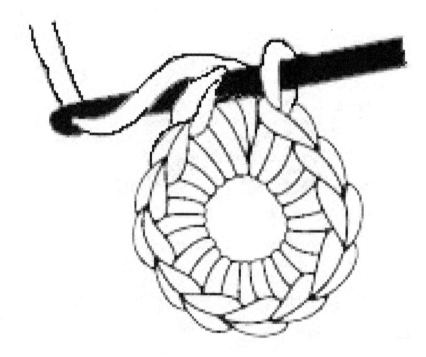

4. Make a slip stitch in the first chain of 3, joining the second circle.

5. Create a half double crochet stitch into the first stitch.

6. Make a double crochet stitch and a triple crochet stitch into this first stitch, which will start to give your first petal shape

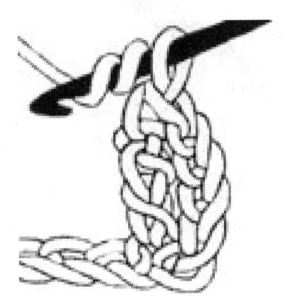

7. In the next stitch, create a treble crochet stitch, a double crochet stitch, and a half double crochet stitch, which will round off your petal.

8. Make a slip stitch in the next stitch.

9. Repeat steps 4 to 8 until you have 5 petals.

Stitches in Reverse

The reverse stitch is sometimes referred to as a crab stitch, which creates a twisted, rounded

edge that's great for finishing off a project. It's done like this:

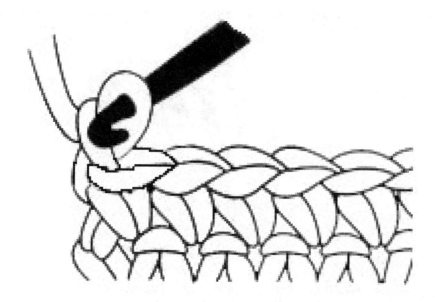

1. Insert your crochet hook from front to back, in the next stitch to the right. Be sure to have the right side of your work facing you.

2. Yarn over and draw the yarn through the stitch in a similar way to how you do a single crochet stitch – just in reverse.

Yarn over and draw the yarn through the 2 loops on your hook, completing one single reverse crochet stitch.

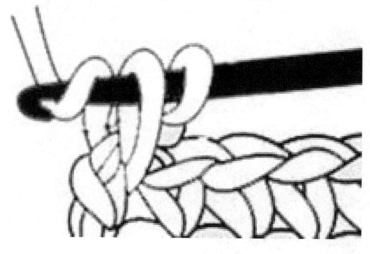

Cluster Stitch

The cluster stitch is made up of several stitches that are half-closed, then joined together as described below.

1. Make a slip knot and create your foundation chain.

2. Yarn over hook, insert hook into the next stitch.

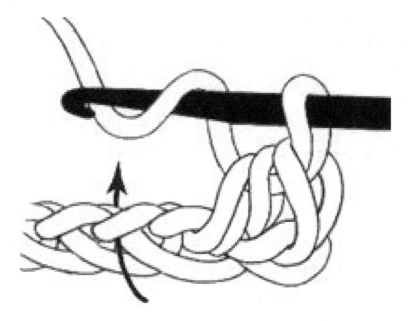

3. Yarn over, draw yarn through the stitch.

4. Yarn over, draw through 2 loops on the hook.

5. Repeat steps 2 to 4 three times.

6. Yarn over and draw through the 5 loops on the hook. This completes a cluster created with 4 double crochet stitches.

Chapter 11: More Techniques and Stitches

Tube Crochet

Crocheting in a tube takes slightly more attention, so go about it carefully. Here are two techniques that you can use for crocheting a tube. Firstly, you can read through the instruction for making a stepped tube. Each of the rounds is crocheted separately, after which the next round is stepped up, so to speak, and worked as another of the tube. The next one you can try is a spiral tube, a continuous method.

The only way to determine which one of these techniques you'll use in the future is to try them. There could be some basic stitches you are confident at doing, and you can choose accordingly. It is good to try both of them, though, because patterns often specify using one or the other.

Stepped Tube

1. Start with a simple slip knot and crochet the number of chain stitches you need. For example, 20 stitches are fine. Just remember not to include the first stitch on your hook when you are counting your stitches.

2. Straighten your chain so the Vs are pointing in the same direction. Insert the crochet hook into your first chain and work on a slip stitch from there. At this point, you have now connected your chain to a tube.

3. Chain the number of stitches that you need to crochet the stitch pattern you are using like you are working in back and forth directions.

4. Finish off your round by working on a slip stitch to the top of the chain at the start of the round. To work the next round, repeat steps 3 to 4 until you have reached the length you require. This method could take some practice but keep at it.

Spiral Tube

This technique will be very valuable should you decide to work on projects such as socks, hats, and items with crocheted arms. These tubes are far simpler to work than the stepped tubes in that they are seamless. So, try out these instructions:

1. Create a foundation chain to work from of the desired length. Join your chain; you can do so by putting your hook into both of your loops of the first stitch so you can make a slip stitch. It is advisable to measure your tube at this point to check the length of it.

2. Now, mark the start of your new round. You are now able to make your second round by working on a

single crochet stitch into every of the chain stitches.

3. Once you have completed the second round, you can make the third round as you work single crochet stitches into each stitch from the previous round.

4. You can repeat this process to complete your tube and end it off nicely with a slip knot. You should snip the yarn at least a few inches away from the slip knot. You can also make use of a yarn needle to insert your loose end into the spiral tube.

Useful hints when making spiral tubes:

- Make sure that you don't loosen or tighten your stitches as you are working.

- Changing the size of your stitches will affect the overall appearance of your tube.

- Track your rounds using a marker; a safety pin is perfect for this. It will help you to keep track of the number of stitches in each round. Once you start a new round, move your marker.

Mesh and Trellis Work

Mesh and trellis techniques produce lace patterns that can be used for numerous items.

Basic Mesh Technique

Proceed as follows:

1. Prepare your base chain with an odd number of stitches. For example, 11 stitches.

2. Next, work a row of 10 single chain stitches and make 3 chain stitches at the end and turn. Now skip the first stitch and work into the next stitch creating a slip stitch.

3. Next, make 3 chain stitches, skip the next stitch, make a stitch and, after that, make a slip stitch. Repeat these steps as you work across the row; remember to turn after every row, and you'll end up with a lovely mesh pattern.

Basic Trellis Technique

The chain spaces in the trellis-work are larger and form arches giving it a more attractive look. Try the following steps:

1. Make a foundation chain. Your stitches should be in multiples of 4 plus an additional 2 stitches.

2. Row one: Work on the single-chain into six chain stitches from your hook. *Still in row 1, make five chain stitches, skip three chain stitches, work one of your single crochet to the following chain.* Repeat this from *till the end of the chain.

3. Row two: *Make 5 chain stitches, then work 1 single chain into the next 5 chain space. Repeat from *until the end of your row.

You can repeat the second row as many times as you need to until you are complete, then fasten off.

Embellishments for Crochet Surfaces

Surface Slipstitch

1. First, make a slip knot on your hook. Be sure the right side of the crocheted surface is facing upwards, and insert your hook into a space between the stitches. You can decide where to insert it, and then draw a loop of different yarn through.

2. Then stick your hook into the next space that is between two stitches and draw up the loop through the loop that is on the hook.

3. Repeat this until the end of the pattern.

You should have a lovely row of different colored slip stitches on the surface of your work.

Surface Knots

1. Cut your yarn according to the length you require, and then you should make a slip knot on your hook.

2. Once again, with the right side of your surfacing facing upwards, insert your hook under one of the stitch loops and pull through a loop of new yarn.

3. Make one chain stitch; then, you should yarn it over and stick the hook under that same loop on your surface. Do these steps again until you make the knot as big as you want it to be.

4. Then you should yarn over and pass it through all the loops on the hook and close it with a slip stitch.

5. Pull the remaining yarn through and bring the tail to the wrong side of the surface.

How to Crochet Beads into Your Surface

1. Firstly, decide how many beads you'll need for your pattern and then thread them through your yarn. You must thread the beads before proceeding. If you are using a variety of beads, thread them from the last bead, which you'll need to the first, make a slip knot with your yarn. The wrong side should be facing upwards, now put in your hook at the back loop of a stitch. You should yarn over and pull through the yarn. At this stage, you have two loops. Beads are added after every alternate row on the wrong side.

2. Slide the bead against the two loops, yarn over (wrap it over the far side of the bead) and pass the yarn through both of these loops. The bead is now secured on the wrong side.

3. Thread your required number of sequins onto your yarn. It is always a good idea to add on a few extra in case you miscounted; you won't need to cut and join your yarn later on if you need to add any. If you are using concave sequins, thread them with the hollow side facing the yarn. Crochet the sequins in the row on the wrong side so that they appear at the back, which is the right side of the surface.

Braids

Braids can be crocheted and sewn on or even thread through mesh surfaces. Here are two lovely braids to try. The shell braid is simple yet elegant, and the double braid, as the name suggests, is fairly broader.

Shell Braid

Begin with four chain stitches, and then you should join them into a ring form with a slip stitch in the first stitch.

Row1: Make three chain stitches, then two double chains in a ring, two chain stitches after that, finally three double chain stitches in a ring, turn your work.

Row2: Make a slip stitch over the following two double chain stitches, then work on a single stitch into a two-chain space, then work on the three chain stitches. Next, work on the following sequence, two double chains, two chains, three double chains; work this sequence into a two- chain space and then turn your work.

Repeat the second row until you reach your desired length and then fasten off neatly.

Double Braid

This braid is crocheted on both sides of the chain.

Start with a foundation chain with a multiple of two stitches, as long as you need.

Row 1: Work on the one double chain into your sixth chain from your crochet hook. * make one chain, skip one chain, work one double chain in the following chain.* Repeat this from * until the end of your current row and turn.

Row2: *Make three chains, then work this sequence (one double chain, three chains, two double chains) into the first one chain space*. Then work through one single crochet in the following space, work (2 double chains, three chains, two double chains) into the next space. Repeat from * until the ending of the row. Repeat row two on the other side of row 1.

Row1 or 2 could be crocheted in a contrasting color, and you could also thread a ribbon through it if you like. Then fasten off.

Hairpin Crochet

This type of crochet is done on a hairpin fork, which can be purchased in various sizes. It is typically used for blankets, shawls, scarves, and also baby clothes. It is something different, so why not give it a try?

1. Hold the hairpin fork in such a way that the curve is at the top.

2. Then proceed to make a slip loop and slip it over the left prong and slide it to the center of the hairpin fork.

3. Hold your hook in the middle of the fork, then yarn over and pass a loop through on the crochet hook.

4. You should yarn over again and pull through the loop on the hook.

5. Then raise your hook vertically, and then turn it left, which is clockwise, so the yarn is curled around the right prong.

6. Insert the hook in the front, which is the left prong. Wrap the yarn on the hook and pull it through. There are only two loops on your hook at this point.

7. Again, yarn over and pull it through both of these loops. Do over steps 5 to 7 till the fork is filled.

8. Once the fork has been filled, remove the bar, and then slip off except the last remaining loops. Next, replace the bar and then repeat steps 5 to 7 until you have the length you require.

9. Next, pass the yarn through the last loops and slide the strip off the fork.

10. Single crochet stitches can be worked into the loops to finish it off. Then, make a slip loop and put the hook into the first loop. Make a double crochet stitch and keep the loops curved the way they come from the fork. Then, make single crochet stitches in every loop till the end of the row. Finally, fasten off and do the same with the loops on the other side.

Button holes and Loops

Horizontal Button holes

Horizontal button holes are used mainly for small pockets, jerseys with button holes on the shoulder, or button hole strips. These follow a very simple method, as follows:

1. Place pins or markers on your work where your button holes need to be made. Be sure to mark the size of the button hole as well.

2. Crochet up to the first marker and make a few chain stitches. The number depends on how many stitches you need to skip to form the button hole.

3. Crochet as usual according to the pattern and repeat the previous steps at each marker. Be sure to skip the same number of stitches for every button hole.

4. In the next row, crochet the pattern over the stitches, making sure that you crochet the same number of stitches that you skipped.

Vertical Buttonholes

These button holes are used when there are no front plackets on a garment.

Follow the steps until you get to the row where the bottom of the button hole will be (in this case, single crochet stitches are used).

1. Make a turning chain for the new row, then three single crochet stitches and turn the work. Leave the remaining stitches.

2. Make a turning chain and single crochet stitches in every stitch and turn.

3. Fasten off the yarn and with the right side facing, skip one single crochet stitch and re join the yarn on the other side to start making the second side of the button hole.

4. Make one chain stitch and also a single crochet stitch in every stitch across the remainder of the front

and turn.

5. Work three more rows of single crochet stitches across, ending with a row on the wrong side top of the button hole.

6. Chain one stitch, skip the space for the button hole, and make single crochet stitches in every one of the next 3 single crochet stitches on the first side of the button hole.

Edgings

Creating edgings to finish off your projects adds a neat finish. There are numerous edgings you can make which involve the use of basic stitches. It is a good idea to try a couple just to get a feel for it, and then you can make other variations using different stitches when you decide to make your edgings.

Simple Edging

Let's try a simple one:

You'll need to crochet five rows for this edging.

Begin with a foundation chain, which should be in four multiples, for example, 20 stitches. **Row1:** Do a single chain into the second chain from your hook, then one single crochet in each chain after that.

Rows2-4: Work one chain stitch, then one single crochet in every Ch stitch until the row's end.

Row5: Work three chain stitches, then skip one single crochet, then work one double chain into the following single chain, work 3 chain stitches, then work 3 double chain stitches over the double chain you've just made. *Skip three single crochet stitches, work one double chain into the next double chain, crochet 3 chain stitches, then 3 double chain stitches over the double chain you just made, repeat from *until the end but finish the row with the following: one single chain, then one double crochet into the last single crochet. After all that, you can fasten off your work.

Crab Stitch Edgings:

You can't go wrong with this edging; it is easy to make and also rather versatile and hardy. Try it and see how it goes; it is practically the same as doing single crochet, the only difference being that you'll be working from left to right as you crochet.

Simple Instructions to Follow:

1. Join the yarn you have to the first stitch, and then draw a loop.

2. Using your crochet hook, turn it around so it inserts into the stitch on the right instead of the left.

3. Your hook should be on the other side now, and you'll need to adjust it so that you draw your working yarn through. The hook should point in a downwards direction to make it easier to hook the yarn.

4. At this point, you should have two loops. Next, you should yarn over and draw in both loops as you did before.

5. And that is one crab stitch completed.

6. Your hook needs to be turned backward now so you can stick it into your stitch, which is to your right. And now, you can repeat steps 3 to 5 once again. Carry on and finish your round.

7. Once you come to the start, you should turn your crochet hook, and then put it into the exact place where you made your first chain stitch.

8. Now, complete the crab stitch, then finish fastening off.

9. Crochet in your loose end on the wrong side of your work for a few cm before cutting the yarn.

Chapter 12. Left Hander's Crochet

Being a left-handed crocheter is a unique thing because you will operate against the current status quo of things. This was due to the fact left-handed crocheters had to draw their knowledge from right-handed crocheters. Thinking about this is a little bit hard for left-handed crocheters. You can imagine learning a skill from an individual who does not have an understanding of it. Well, that's in the past.

Today, the situation is different, as left-handed crocheters have a vast number of sources where they can draw their knowledge from. These sources include various tutorials, patterns, and teachers who have brought themselves to spread the mastery of this art.

When we talk about left-handed crocheting, this is almost as mimicking right-handed crocheting. This is because left-handed crocheting borrows a lot from right-handed crocheting. It can almost seem like a reflection of the other.

The left-handed crocheter, just as the name suggests, will hold his or her crochet on the left hand while the right-handed one will make sure that the crochet is on his or her right-hand side. There are various grips that one may assume when holding the hook. This includes the knife grip or the pencil grip. When this happens, the crocheter may manipulate the hook in whichever way he or she desires.

With left-hander crochets, learning the basics and following the patterns of crocheting is subtle. This is because they are going out of their way in order to learn the mastery of what they have not been doing on a daily basis. Moreover, many crocheting patterns follow the direction of right-handed patterns.

In order to make this less subtle for you as a left-handed crocheter, you need to learn the basis of left-handed crocheting. Below are the various steps which can be very helpful when beginning left-handed crocheting or when maintaining its perfection.

The Hook Should Be in Your Left Hand

Crocheting left-handed will mean you will have to put the crochet in your left hand. This way, your right hand will have the leeway to support the work that you are manipulating. The hook has a flat part that is key when manipulating your work. When you are running the task, your thumb and finger should be on the grip of the flat part of the hook. Holding the crochet properly is key when it comes to effective sewing. The grip of the crochet should be maintained and balanced all through your sewing.

Chaining

The foundation of crocheting begins with this stage. When you are engaging in a crochet project for the first time, you will need to practice chaining. One of the less subtle techniques in crocheting is this one. In order to achieve this, you need to commence by making sure you loop the yarn on your finger. This is often done twice. Your finger here meaning the "index finger". After you have achieved this, the next step will be that you will gently pull your second loop through the first loop.

The result of this is what we call a slip-stitch. After this is achieved, you will need to make sure that you slide the loop that is on your hook with and loop it too. After this, you free the end of the yarn over the hook. In order to make another loop, you need to slide a novel yarn all the way through the loop that was already in existent.

In order to make sure that the number of chains is increasing, you need to carry out this activity in a continuous manner. This way, you will find that you have achieved a chain. Forming a chain is the most basic stance of crocheting since you are carrying out this activity in a continuous manner. The chain should only be limited to the purposes of your project. When in demotion, chaining is often referred to by the abbreviation "ch."

Slip Stitching

A slip-stitch, as it is known, can also be referred to as a stitch that is jointed. The process of slip stitching is one that involves the insertion of the hook through the stitch. After this has been achieved, you will need to proceed to yarn over. In order to complete the formation of the slip- stitch, you will need to you need or make sure that the novel yarn passes through the stitch. With this at hand, you have accomplished the slip-stitch. With a slip-stitch, you can be able to move from one point to another. It can also be used as a link between two stitches. Linking two stitches is of key importance, for instance, when you are making around while crocheting.

Single Crochet

This is a type of stitch which comes as a result of patterns. In order to achieve this type of stitch, you will first need to make sure that the hook goes through the stitch and then make sure that the yarn passes through both stitches. After you have accomplished this, you will need to make sure your yarn is over. This then involves the yarn being pulled through both the loops in a bid to hook it. When abbreviating a single stitch of crochet, this is often denoted as "SC."

Double Crochet

After you have achieved a single crochet, the next step will involve that you do a double crochet. These are other types of crochets that are also common. When double crocheting, you will need to yarn over twice in order to bring about the double effect. Yarning the second time will involve that you insert the hook through the stitch first before you a yarn.

After this has been achieved, you already have the first stitch. With this stitch in place, you need to pull through this stitch and then yarn. You have two stitches in place, and thus you can proceed to pull the hook through them and then yarning again. After pulling through the last two stitches, this will see to it that you get done with the stitch. When denoting double crochet, this is done by a denotation of "dc."

Half-Double Crochet

This type of stitch is not commonly known. Despite this, it is important we get to know this type of stitch. This is because when engaging in a type of work that is more complex in nature, you will need to employ the use of this particular type of stitch. In order to achieve this type of stitch, you need to yarn over, after which you then make sure that the hook goes into the stitch. After you have achieved this, you will need to yarn once more over this time you are pulling through a number of stitches. It could be three. Half double crochet is often denoted as "hdc."

Triple Crochet

With knowledge of single and double crochet in mind, you will now need to focus on acquiring the knowledge of triple crochet. In order to achieve a triple crochet, your first move will be to yarn over twice. This way, you are in a position to make sure that the hook goes into the stitch and that you can yarn over once more.

After you have achieved this, you will need to pull this yarn through the existing four loops. With this in place, you will further need to pull the hook over through two loops, after which you will then have to yarn once more. In order to finish the stitch, you will have to consider pulling through the final two loops. When denoting this type of stitch, you will do so in a manner that suggests the formation of a "tr."

Crocheting in a Circle

When carrying out this particular type of drill as a left-handed, it will follow the same path as it would when you are right-handed. We have already gathered how to make a chain, which will be your first order of events. In order to crochet in a circle, you will first need to make a chain. You have already gathered how a slip-stitch works, and so after you have achieved a chin, you will need to gather it at the center by using a slip-stitch. When you have already achieved this, you are in a position to advance in your chain making. Crocheting in the round is an effective way to make heavy-scarves, cowls, and hats.

Try Out Various Special Stitches

When crocheting, you can assume various different patterns that come in handy when you want to create something captivating. We have already had a feel of what basic stitches entail, and in order to comprehend more complex stitches, we will first need to have an understanding of the basic stitches. Apart from the basic stitches we have already gathered, there exist other types of stitches that come in handy when creating something interesting. These types of stitches include pop-corn stitch, box stitch, and shell stitch.

As a left-handed, there are a number of things that will stand out when seeking to put up with apt crocheting. Some of these factors include:

Left-Handed Tutorials

Crocheting is a practical venture. When indulging in crocheting for the first time, you will need to have as much practical assistance as possible. With reference pictures, you are in a position to effectively understand the formation of a particular type of stitch. This is because you are able to see it as it forms. Learning how to crochet is an uphill task, especially for left-handed individuals. The net is filled with a lot of tutorials that are on crocheting using the left hand. An individual may use this when seeking out crocheting. With a tutorial, you are blowing to follow through the whole process of crocheting all the way to your success.

This is because you can pause and rewind where you might not have captured correctly. Moreover, there are blogs of other left-handed crocheters that are inexistence. Following them and acquiring knowledge from them is easier because they tend to relate to you. There are also left-handed crocheters books. These books are various in the market, and thus you can choose to settle on one that will work best for you.

Following the Pattern to the Letter

Left-handed crocheting entails that you encompass the same patterns that a right-handed crocheter would use. When you have a pattern for right-handed crocheters, you will follow the pattern to the letter only to use your left hand when doing this. This also means that you can use many right-handed tutorials to your advantage.

You may be watching a tutorial for right-handed crocheters, but when you follow through with your left hand, you will find that you achieve the same results. As a result, you find that right- hand crocheters and left-handed crocheters are one and the same. The only distinction is that one uses the right hand, whereas the other uses the help of his or her left hand.

Flipping Pictures and Images

Most left-handed individuals refrain from right-handed tutorials not because they cannot work in benefit of them but because of their already formed perception about this kind of tutorials. In order to make sure this perception is eradicated from left-handed individuals, a left-handed individual ought to assume patterns and ways that will work to their advantage. One of the most tactful procedures a left-handed may adopt in a bid to secure a deeper comprehension of patterns is by taking them and inverting them. When you invert a picture that was taken by a right-handed individual, you will find that it appears as if it is from a left-handed individual. There are a number of points to note when dealing with the left-handed crocheting. For instance, you need to leave your beginning yarning tail hanging. This should be done at the beginning of every project; its essence is deep-rooted to the instance that you should not crochet over it. The tails come in handy when creating a cue, whether you are on the right- hand side of the cue or the left-hand side.
The right side always manifests itself at the right bottom corner. Another point to note for left-handed crocheters is that every time you are adopting a position of yarning over, you are doing this in a clockwise manner. You need to master this move as this is what makes sense to the whole process of crocheting.

The rear numerous patterns for left-handed crocheters; this may involve the written one sand also the visible ones that are visual. Although the visible ones seem easier, left-handed crocheting is possible for both types of crocheting.

This is because a crocheter is being asked to relay what is in the written or what is in the book to what he or she is actually engaging in. A pattern that has been written down can easily be followed through just by the use of cognitive awareness that for left-handed, the direction of the yarn will be a little different. There are various types of patterns which in order to work best, need to be reversed in order to be implemented with ease. For instance, there is a type of crochet pattern known as the tapestry pattern that requires reversing in order for it to work properly. There are also other patterns known color work patterns that require a reversal in order for them to function properly.

When you reverse filet crochet, one that is used when writing words, you are in a position to read the letters that were written in a manner that is reversed. When a left-handed does not work on reversing this particular type of work, you will find that this creates confusion on the rows and the stitches.

Often, the expected outcome will not arrive because of the mismatch in the various rows and stitches. With symbol charts, this is directed to right-handed crochets. Owing to this fact, left-handed crocheters ought to follow the same drill as depicted in the symbol charts but in a manner that is opposing to the already depicted symbol.

This means that you will adopt the symbol but mean opposite manner. Reversing a pattern can be done in the consciousness of an individual. This entails the individual forming a picture in his or her head and in turn, reversing it. If you cannot do this, the best way to reverse the pattern would be by using a mirror.

Chapter 13: Common Crochet Mistakes and How to Avoid Them

Stitch markers look like such a headache. Significant and also dangly ones get in your way. Tiny ones might not glide smoothly on big needles. They all take some time to put on the needles and also add an added action to relocate them while weaving stitches. After that, why utilize them? They form a pointer while you knit.

From simple garter stitch to difficult shoelace, stitch markers advise a knitter that some kind of various requirement needs to happen. When switching over to a different yarn, a brand-new stitch, or a pattern repeat, a marker states, "Hey, take note here."

When first learning to knit, starting knitters get lost in the methods, the stitches, the feel of the yarn, and more. Utilizing a marker provides a beginner knitter back to the facts, back to considering the pattern to determine what comes next, even directly back to putting those last couple of stitches in to develop a beautiful boundary.

When I initially learned to knit, I made the common mistake of not making use of markers. I assumed that as long as I adhered to the pattern, every little thing would work out great. Well, it didn't. If the design called for the same kind of stitch in the pattern, however, various one for the boundary, I occasionally kept knitting the pattern stitch to the end of the row.

My mistakes didn't show up until I weaved a whole lot more rows. As I had not yet found out how to undo stitches without removing rows, I needed to choose between eliminating several rows or leaving the mistake in the item. In some circumstances, I did not find the errors until impeding the piece far too late after that.

How to Fix It Correctly

If the pattern does not call for putting markers, there is no reason you shouldn't work without them. Try putting markers at the start or end of pattern repeats, right after or right before a border side, at a sign up with when knitting in the round, or at a color modification for Fair Isle knitting. All are good options and it is up to you to select which ones work best for you.

If you fail to remember to add a marker while knitting a row, you can include a pen by using a stitch marker, which is available to move over the needle. Additional alternative needles are running a small item of thread between the stitches and over the needle. Make a knot in the loop. On the following row, slip the thread as you would with a metal or plastic marker or replace it with one of those.

Fora task with a lot of rows, stitch markers function similarly well for counting rows. Utilize a piece of contrasting cotton yarn or a yarn that won't leave little bits and also parts of fiber behind when gotten rid of. Take a tiny part, connect a knot, and slip it over your needle before finishing a row. Knit a set variety of rows, such as 5 or 10, and add another marker. Clip out when all set for ending your completed job.

If you neglect to add one of these little markers, thread a needle with cotton yarn and also carefully run it via a stitch. Make a knot in the string, and you have one more marker. The markers that open and close make a great additional option for keeping track of rows. These could be included while knitting the row or after.

Mistake 2: Picking the Incorrect Cast-On

Externally, every cast-on does the same thing by creating loops on a needle that gets dropped off by drawing yarn through them with a second needle. However, a standard knitting error made by several beginners can be to choose the incorrect cast-on for a task or to alter the cast-on recommended by the pattern developer.

Each type of cast-on has a function beyond developing those first loops. A cast-on sets the phase for the garment. For instance, when casting-on stitches for the leg opening of a sock, the wrong cast-on can make it a fight to get the sock on over your foot, or worse, it can trigger the top to fall around your ankles.

Cast-on either offers the edge of your job both stretch and elasticity or just sufficient stretch for putting it on while sustaining the continuing to be stitched in the garment. When you make use of an elastic cast-on, such as a weaved cast-on, the edge of your project will relocate conveniently.

Nonetheless, if you utilize this type of cast-on for something like the neck of a gown that you wish to lie level, it may not support the stitches in the corset, causing it to gap open rather than stay flat against your skin.

The Fix

If a pattern does not state which cast-onto use, numerous knowledgeable knitters use the long-tail cast-on as their go-to cast-on. Moderately stretchy with a tip of the framework, the long tail-cast on help a lot of pieces of work.

If the cast-on looks too limited, removing and beginning again with a various one may be your most beautiful. Believe me. I've done this more frequently than I like to confess, but obtaining the cast-on right makes the rest of the project job far better.

If the builder selected a particular cast-on, however, your cast-on side features too much over all flexibility, try out casting-on with an inferior sized needle, next proceed to the needle required in the pattern to start your very first row. Alternatively, if the cast-on has excessive structure, cast-on with a bigger sized needle, and then move to the appropriate size for the very first row.

If the job has way too much elasticity at the cast-on edge, usage progressed, there are finishing methods to add definition to the side.

Mistake 3: Binding Off Too Tightly

The tension utilized when binding off helps give form to your work. When you bind off stitches as well snugly, some facts take place.

It makes obstructing your process to the perfect measurements harder, normally impossible since a restricted bind off squeezes your stitches towards the biggest part of the job.

Your cast-on for a toe-up sock might be excellent; however, if you bind off the leg opening tightly, good luck getting that sock very our ankle joint. The same fact occurs for neck or wrist openings.

It makes an inflexible straight side that doesn't feel or look good, which frequently contrasts with the soft qualities of the rest of the job.

If you commonly knit with tighter stress, move your stitches to a needle 1 to 2 dimensions larger than used for the job. Bind off with the larger sized needles.

If you typically maintain tension by wrapping the working yarn around your fingers while knitting, drop it for the bind off. Instead, freely drape the working yarn over one finger or between 2 fingers for taking in the stitch. Allow they are to move over or between your fingers to stay clear of the extra stress.

If you knit within the American or United Kingdom style, keep the yarn in the middle of your fingers, as well as wrap it freely around the needle to make the bind off stitch without drawing it as tight as you would certainly for a typical knit or purl stitch.

Most significantly, inspect the tension after the last bind off stitch and before you reduced the yarn. If it also looks tight, meticulously unpick the stitches, putting the stitches back on a needle, and redo the bind off. Yes, I've done this too.

Mistake 4: Selecting the Wrong Yarn for a Project

Whether knitting from your very own design or from a pattern created by somebody else, choosing the right yarn for the task helps ensure the garment turns out lovely.

In some cases, you do intend to see if a dimension 80 tatting cotton thread knits just like gossamer Shet land. And that's a high point to do since testing when knitting creates enjoyable times.

Nevertheless, using the right yarn does have an objective: recognizing exactly how different threads drape, lose, knit-up, tablet make a distinction. Besides, yarn weight and color contribute to the yarn option.

When a coat pattern requires a DK weight merino wool, and you pick a fingering weight alpaca, not only will the gauge be off, but the sleeves and the sweater will pool at your wrists and mid section, respectively, because alpaca's soft fibers drape higher than wool. Possibly you desire that appearance, yet if not, why waste the initiative?

Changing the fiber also impacts the garment. The majority of pet fibers have a halo, with mohair and angora revealing the most halo. These fuzzy tendrils of the texture add extra warmth to a weaved garment. When selecting them for a shoe lace task, the halo hides a lot of the pattern.

Garments that are required to stretch, such as for example gloves and socks, won't take just as much if knitted with materials such as silk or bamboo. When using dark tinted yarns, stitches become low-key or shed, especially when knitting lace or any pattern with twisted stitches.

The Fix

When selecting yarn not asked for in a pattern, check out the yarn tag. Reference the yarn weight and the producer's suggested needle dimension if it suits the pattern's yarn weight and needle sizing. When the yarn coincides or identical fiber, from then on, the thread must operate within the project.

When weaving lace and you intend to use fiber that creates a halo, select a pattern with an even more open job. The stitches will undoubtedly be extra defined with a mild misty radiance from the halo rather than getting shed in all that fuzz.

Further more, when knitting a shoe lace, select lighter tinted threads if you desire the shoe lace lay out to be a prominent attribute. When utilizing dark-colored yarns, the adverse room of the open holes ends up being noticeable feature. Pick which style you wish to see in the completed garment.

If you wish to use silk yarn when the pattern asks for wool, you must rework the gauge and view the stitch tension. Without woolen's elasticity, silk yarn knits-up with even more structure and less bounce, which implies a garment might have a tighter fit.

Mistake 5: Starting a Project Without Swatching

The scourge of lots of a knitter's existence, a swatch makes lots of points for knitters of any experience level. It shows if the yarn you've picked helps the job. Its hows if you are knitting to assess, which suggests if you'll have sufficient yarn to finish the task, and also if you require to read just for sizing. It likewise shows the pattern, which lets you understand if you have selected an excellent yarn color.

Various other advantages of Swatching consist of:

Learning if the dyer established the dye appropriately (If they did not, the color would run when you dampen the swatch for obstructing).

Enquiring if the pattern and yarn block well.

Learning if you like the pattern to determine if you need to proceed with the task.

The Fix

Make as watch per the pattern directions if the pattern doesn't consist of as watch size; after that, select one that's four times as big as the gauge. For example, if the design asks for four stitches to 1 inch over four rows, after that knit as watch that has at the very least 16 stitches, as well as 16 rows.

The added stitches and rows give you more to obstruct and will also show you just how the item looks.

Mistake 6: Knitting Without a Lifeline

Iassume, perhaps, it is one of the most discouraging of all the usual knitting blunders, despite how much time you've been knitting.

It happens to all knitters, yet more so for beginners - stitches get dropped, incorrect stitches get made, and knitting enjoyment becomes ripping out your work or tossing it apart in irritation.

You can remove each row from the beginning, seeking your LYS for aid. Or you can opt for a natural solution that experienced knitters use.

The Fix

Although not always so crucial if working a garter or a stockinet stitch, a lifeline offers you the aid when stitches or patterns are extra detailed

Thread a needle with cotton thread and even dental floss, and also run the needle and string with the stitches on your needle. Have the thread be a few inches much longer than the width of the knitted row. Gather the stitches for the following row without catching the lifeline in the stitches. If you do find a couple of stitches, do not fret, as the guideline draws through the work when you give it a mild yank.

Some round and interchangeable needles feature a lifeline opening pre-drilled in the connect cord. Insert the support via the hole, and then begin weaving. The stitches go back across the support-line minus the extra function of the reading the help-line while using stitches having a needle.

Should you choose to rip out several rows, you need to rip back to the support-line. Fewer rows removed indicate you can get back to weaving, so I occasionally utilize 3 or 4 support-lines as I knit a job. It offers me the alternative of ripping back even more rows if required.

Mistake 7: Knitting Without Counting

Have you ever before shed your location in a chart or a set of composed instructions? Have you ever back dropped stitches without understanding it?

I did not count stitches continuously; however, the frustration of functioning a row and winding up with way too many or otherwise sufficient stitches becomes frustrating. Whether I knitted expensive shoelace shawls or an essential one shade hat, my attention would wander, and I would have problems. Now I know not to make this standard knitting error.

Whatever concerning knitting can be over whelming to a beginner knitter. There seem so many things to learn and bear in mind. Counting stitches as you work doesn't appear to supply much aid, and it does take a bit of additional time; it makes knitting a lot less complicated! You'll rapidly recognize if you've dropped a stitch or knit the wrong stitch, such as a k2 Tog when a k2 Was called for, or accidentally added an added yarn over.

To save a period when counting, subject in sets of 2 or 5 stitches; this uncomplicated technique is effective. When you have plenty of stitches to cast-on, use sew pensat specific periods, such as every 10 or 20 stitches. This helpful idea keeps you from counting and stating thousands of cast-on loops. You can swiftly count these fewer stitches before casting-on more to guarantee you put sufficient stitches on your needle.

You can make counting stitches for detailed patterns less complicated by counting the variety of stitches in each pattern row. When a design requires increases or decreases that always change the type of stitches per row, count the variety of stitches in the chart or written guidelines for each row. Understanding precisely the number of stitches in each row helps you recognize if you have actually raised or lowered correctly.

Mistake 8: Starting a Project without Reading Through the Pattern

Beginner and veteran knitters like starting up brand-new projects. Itching to get our palms around a couple of fine needles, we cast-on and begin weaving the pattern as soon as we can. However, reviewing a design from beginning to end remains one of the crucial distinctions between smart and knowledgeable knitters, and it's also

95

a typical error that beginning knitters typically make.

Why is reading via a pattern vital?

Each pattern designer creates differently.

Publishers wish to take advantage of space and several area's notes or unique methods in many areas of a pattern, not merely at the beginning.

Innovative stitches need new signs in a chart that you may not have knitted before. Recognizing if or when you need to alter needles allows you to be careful when it occurs in the pattern.

When knitting a color job, knowing if you lug the yarn throughout the work or up the side keeps your work clean.

If the design requires sliding the initial stitch, nevertheless, you opt to knit it as an alternative, recognizing in advance that you'll grab and also knit that stitch later in the pattern will certainly make a difference in the look of your finished piece.

The Fix

Check out the pattern from beginning to finish before you start. Ensure you understand precisely how to knit it, how to do the stitches, and that you have all the materials you require.

Chapter 14: Some Crochet Patterns for All Abilities

Basic Stitches

This is designed to give you some of the most basic crochet stitches that are very beginner-friendly. You can use these stitches for entire projects or the basis of these stitches as a frame for more advanced stitches found later in this guide.

Single Crochet

When learning how to crochet, single crochet will become your best friend. It is the core stitch you will need to learn because it is incorporated into many crochet patterns you will come across. The single crochet has the appearance of a very tight piece of fabric. It has very few holes in it and has distinctive uniform rows that look elegant and crisp. This gives your work a very clean look. Height-wise, single crochet is one of the smallest of the crochet stitches; therefore, work tends to build slowly when using this stitch.

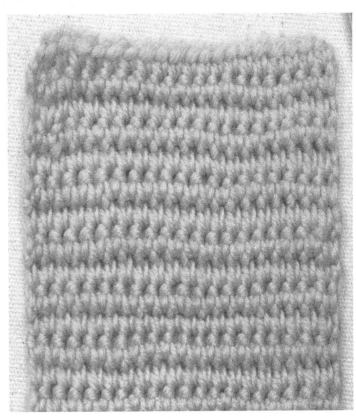

To single crochet, begin with your chain or row; insert your crochet hook into the next stitch or chain along. Put your yarn over your hook and draw that yarn through the hole. Once you have brought the yarn through the stitch or chain, you should now have 2 loops on your hook. Yarn over again and draw that yarn through both of these loops on your hook. You should now be left with only 1 loop on your hook, and that is it! That is how simple single crochet is.

Slip Stitch

A slip stitch, like the single crochet, is one of the basics. It has a huge variety of uses and it is crucial to learn early. A row of slip stitches looks very uniform and tight. This stitch is not typically used for large sheets of fabric or objects due to how tightness of the stitches. The most common use for this stitch is for crossing a row without adding any more height to your work. It is also used to make something tighter, such as the rim of a hat. Slip stitches are commonly used to join two bits of work together, such as two sheets of fabric; to do this; you work a slip stitch through both pieces of fabric to join them together.

Double Crochet

Double crochet is twice the height of single crochet and is just as easy. This crochet stitch has a much more open look, and projects using this stitch will build very quickly. Due to the height of this stitch, you will tend to need a larger starting chain; otherwise, your work can begin to look warped.

To double crochet, begin by yarning over your hook. This will leave you with 2 loops on your hook. Insert the crochet hook into the next stitch (or 3rd stitch if starting at the beginning of a row) and yarn over once more and draw that yarn through the stitch. You will now have 3 loops on your hook. Yarn over a final time, draw the yarn through the last 2 loops on your hook, and you are done.

Advanced Stitches

This will focus on the fiddly and more advanced crochet stitches. The results are unique and unusual stitches you can use in your next project.

Half Double Crochet

This stitch is a variant of double crochet. The height of this stitch is the hallway between single and double crochet. This stitch has fewer steps than double crochet, which makes it a favorite among many people. Another significant attribute of this stitch is that it is tall like double crochet, but has the density of single crochet.

To make half double crochet, begin by yarning over your hook. This will leave you with 2 loops on your hook. Insert the crochet hook into the next stitch and yarn over once more and draw that yarn through the stitch. You will now have 3 loops on your hook. At this point, all of these steps are the same as double crochet; it is how you finish the different stitch.

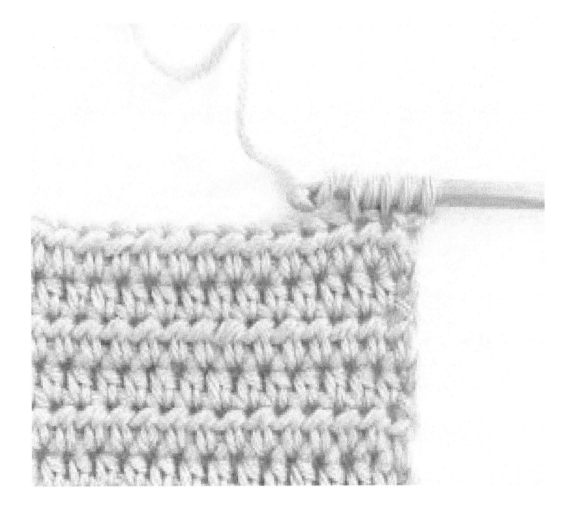

Treble Crochet

Treble crochet is a very tall stitch. It is commonly used for large open projects such as lightweight blankets. This stitch does require quite a few steps, but once you have mastered how to do this, it will not take very long at all. As with double crochet, you will need to compensate when turning your work by chaining 3-5 depending on the pattern.

Yarn over and pull through 2 of the 4

Loops on your hook, you will be left with 3 loops after pulling through. Yarn over again and pull through another 2 loops; you will be left with 2 loops on your hook. Yarn over a final time and pull through the remaining 2 loops on your hook.

Yes, it is a bit time-consuming and tricky to work with, but the results are worth it.

A great way to remember how many times to pull through the loops is in the names. Single crochet only pulls through the loops once; double crochet pulls through the loops twice, and the treble crochet will pull through the loops three times.

Front Post Double Crochet

The front post double crochet can be tricky to learn, especially if you are new to crochet. The confusion comes from the placement of your hook. The front post double crochet is simply regular double crochet, but what makes it unique is where you will place your hook before beginning this stitch.

The finished stitch will give you the effect of a raised edge or ridge through your

work. When used in conjunction with a back post double crochet, it can create a beautiful pattern.

To begin, do a standard row of double crochet; this is your foundation for this stitch. If the foundation is not done, the stitch will not work. Chain 2 when you reach the end of this row. At the beginning of your new row, yarn over, and instead of inserting your hook into the top of the double crochet stitch, go under and around the stitch or post itself as shown.

Now yarn over and pull the yarn through the way you came. Finish off with regular double crochet by yarning over and going through 2 loops, yarning over and going through the final 2 loops.

Back-Post Double Crochet

Like the front post double crochet, this is simply glorified double crochet but put into a different place to create a unique little design in your work. This stitch can be used by itself or in conjunction with the front post double crochet to create a fun raised and sunken texture within your projects.

To begin, do a regular row of double crochet to form the foundation for this stitch, chain 2 at the end of your row for turning.

Now yarn over and instead of going into

At the top of the stitch, go behind your work and insert your hook around the post of the stitch as shown. From this position, yarn over and pull the yarn through the path which you came to draw up a loop.

The front and back post double crochet work very well together and can create a type of stitch known as a basketweave, covered later on in this guide. These two stitches are also a perfect example of how you can take a regular basic stitch like the double crochet and alter it slightly to give you a great effect.

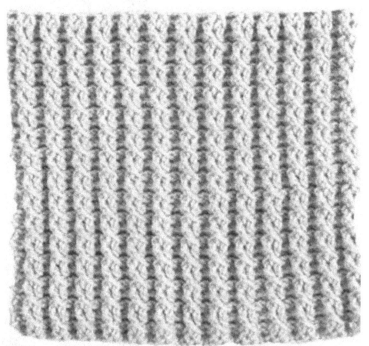

Textured Stitches

This will focus on textured stitches. There are a wide variety of crochet stitches that give great textures through fairly simple methods; these have been areas on crochet that have become so popular. The stitches are relatively easy to complete, and some of them are just an expansion of stitches

Front Loop Crochet

Not to be confused with the similar front post crochet, this stitch is simple and doesn't have much of an impact. The stitch can make your plain objects have a touch of pizzazz with no extra effort, as it utilizes a very basic and user-friendly single crochet.

To begin, you need to see where your crochet hook goes. You can see from the top view of a chain or row of single crochet that you have two distinctive loops. For regular crochet, you would use both of these loops when inserting your hook, however, for front loop crochet you will be going through that first loop closest to you only!

Once at this stage, simply yarn over and pull through. Yarn over and go through both 2 loops on your hook exactly as you would in double crochet; there is nothing more to this stitch, but to make more of them!

Back Loop Crochet

Just like in the front loop crochet, do not get this stitch confused with a back post double crochet as they are 2 different things. Just like the front loop crochet, this stitch utilizes the basic single crochet to create a unique pattern. This particular type of crochet is also used in making items like shoes and containers, as it manipulates the yarn to bend and fold in the required directions.

To begin, first you need to see where your crochet hook goes, you can see from the top view of a chain or row of single crochet that you have two distinctive loops. For regular crochet, you would use both of these loops when inserting your hook. However, for back loop crochet you will be inserting your hook through the back loop only. Once you have done this, yarn over as you would with a single crochet, pull the yarn through, yarn over, and pull through both of the 2 loops on your hook to complete the stitch.

Moss Stitch

The Moss stitch uses 2 different crochet stitches to add a unique look to your work. This is a simple yet intriguing stitch that will spruce up many of your projects.

Begin at the beginning of your row, and start by putting a regular half double crochet in that first stitch and then slip stitch into the next stitch. Repeat this pattern of one half double crochet and one slip stitch to the end of the row. You will be able to see a little dip in your work wherever you did a slip stitch.

Once you reach the end of your row, chain 1, and turn your work. This means wherever you put a half double crochet, you now want to do a slip stitch, and wherever there is a slip stitch, you want to do a half double crochet. If you forget which stitch you are, you can look at the stitch below it. If the stitch below is small than the one next to it then it was a slip stitch; if it is taller than the stitch next to it, then it was a half double crochet. Keep working on this pattern until you are happy with the length of your work.

Basket Stitch

This particular stitch makes use of the stitches covered in advance of this book. It uses both the front and back post double crochet, but in a particular pattern to create a beautiful texture to any pattern.

This type of stitch is mainly used for table runners, hats, and blankets. The reason is that the stitch takes a long time to complete, and the result is a

dense fabric. However, you can experiment with using this stitch in any project you would like. To begin, first start with the correct number of chains because this pattern relies on multiples. This means you must always have enough chains in that multiple. For example, if you decide you want 4 stitches per basket stitch, then your overall number of chains should be a multiple of 4, such as 16. If you wanted 5 stitches, then it would be a multiple of 5, such as 15.

For this demonstration, we will be using a multiple of 4.

1. Begin by having a chain of 16 with an extra 2 for your stitch allowance. Next, put one double crochet in each stitch to the end of the row, chain 2, and turn your work.

2. At this stage, you now want to do 4 back post double crochets and then 4 front post double crochets, repeat this pattern to complete the row, chain 2, and turn.

3. Now repeat the pattern, but this time in reverse. So wherever you put a front post double crochet, put a back post double crochet and vice versa.

4. Simply repeat this pattern until your work is at a length you are happy with.

X Stitch

The X stitch is a very open type of stitch. The reason it is in this book is that it has a wonderful pattern and texture that adds a beautiful highlight to any work. The X stitch, like the other stitches, makes use of the stitches in the basics of this guide. Note that this particular stitch requires knowledge of double crochet.

This stitch is worked over 2 stitches. Be sure your chain or row is an even number so you can fit all the stitches.

-To begin, skip the first stitch and put double crochet into the second stitch. Once you complete the first double crochet, yarn over and insert the hook into the stitch or chain you skipped previously.

This stitch is a little tricky to get your head around in the beginning, but it is well worth the effort as you can add a unique look to your work.

Chapter 15: Teaching a Kid

Teaching a toddler to crochet is a rewarding revel that could have lifelong blessings for the budding crafter.

A lot of us discovered crochet at a completely younger age, and despite the fact we would have dropped it for years at a time, the craft caught round in our reminiscences as something useful.

With advantages in each the fast-term and lengthy-time period, it is a talent worth taking the time to train children of almost any age. However, just how do you move approximately coaching an infant to crochet?

Why Educate an Infant to Crochet: The Advantages

There are a few immediate benefits to teaching an infant to crochet; one of them is that it gives them something thrilling to occupy their hours. Only some short-time period blessings of crocheting include:

- Children are capable of specific their creativity in a new way. Even though crochet is a based craft, it's also widely open to interpretation and desire, giving kids ample possibility for self-expression through color choice and other venture-making selections.
- First, there is the pleasure of gaining knowledge of the way to do something new. Then there's the opportunity of creating purposeful gadgets for self and others, which brings about a lot of delight.
- Crocheting hones motor abilities. Children can also find a hook and yarn craft a little bit unwieldy at the beginning, but as they exercise it, their motor skills will enhance, and the craft will become simpler.
- Crochet also can mean working towards other abilities. Older kids can practice getting to know to examine, following commands, and even simple math via running on crochet styles.
- Crochet is an excellent analog opportunity to spend less time on phones, iPads, and other gadgets.
- Research is beginning to expose that children's developing brains are significantly impacted by way of too many hours spent on displays.
- Reminiscence and interest wane while there may be continually the instant gratification of the Internet.
- Taking time to crochet facilitates a gradual child down and development of one's mind areas that require offline stimulation.

At What Age Can a Toddler Learn How to Crochet?

One of the first questions that dad and mom ask earlier than trying to teach an infant to crochet is whether or not their child is old enough.

There's no specific age at which a child can learn to crochet due to the fact all kids learn at specific paces.

That stated, children can start to learn the fundamentals of crochet around the age of 5, and they can grow to surely work on crochet styles around the age of nine.

That curriculum begins with knitting, around the age of 6, after which progresses to include numerous years of cantered crochet lessons beginning the following year.

Steps to Teaching Kids How Crotchet

All people crochet in their fashion, so the most vital aspect is to check your approach to crochet and try to break down every step right into a chew-sized chew for a kid to learn.

Experience unfastened to evolve the following steps as a result of your fashion and the needs of the child you're coaching:

STEP 1: Allow the Child to Show It as a Hobby First

It's not normally an excellent concept to "force" a craft on a child. What's going to stay with a toddler so much more than the instructional steps is the actual pleasure discovered in crafting. Crochet often around your child and be geared up to train him while he first suggests a few interests on his personal. If that interest isn't approaching, you may make materials available or advocate it as an interest amongst different options.

STEP 2: Dealing With the Materials

In case you do, make certain to consist of only the ones so one can facilitate a toddler's easy getting to know (easy yarn in a solid, mild color, hooks with a comfy grip).

Err on the facet of larger is better — huge hooks and thick yarn. For terribly younger kids - or any child having difficulty using a crochet hook - you can need to attempt finger crochet first.

STEP 3: Mastering the Chain

The first step for kids mastering a way crochet is studying to the chain. You can make the slip knot for them and get the hook installation, and you may even make the first few chains to get them going.

When coaching crochet, you'll need to break everything down into the smallest steps feasible, displaying the child how steps build on every difference to result in a completed assignment. For chaining, the steps are:

- Yarn above
- Seize the yarn with the hook
- Pull through

To teach this, you'll want to sit face-to-face with the kid and display the motions, actually displaying every specific part of this step.

Then watch as they practice. Do not leap in too speedy to "restore" things as they get the grasp of it, but be there to aid them in the event they ask for help.

Much younger children may benefit from having you place your palms on top of theirs to guide the movement. Older youngsters may additionally find that looking at video tutorials enables them to get a better idea of what to do.

STEP 4: First Primary Stitch

As soon as a child has mastered the crochet chain, it is time to learn how to make a crochet stitch.

Some humans advocate beginning with a single crochet stitch at the identical time as others propose beginning with double crochet.

Double crochet is easier because it is less difficult to find the right location to make your next stitch. However, single crochet requires fewer steps to finish the sewing.

Use whichever feels high-quality and try the opposite if it's now not working out.

You could need to make the first row of stitches for your child. That is a way of demonstrating the task.

It is also usually less complex to go right into a stitch (which includes the pinnacle of double crochet) than going right into a sequence.

Even though you should show a child how to get through each loop, it's far more essential for the kid to learn how to make a stitch than see the proper placement of the hook.

This is, in particular, true for younger kids.

Chapter 16: Simple Crochet Projects

Girlie Poncho

Size – 24 months

Materials:

- Yarn – Alize cotton yarn in blue and peach color
- Hook– 4.5mm crochet hooks
- Tapestry needle, scissors
- Stitches used – chain (ch), single crochet (sc), double crochet (dc), frontpost double crochet (fpdc), backpost double crochet (bpdc), slip stitch (sl st), st (stitch), [..] total number of stitches

Directions:

Start from the neck while using blue color yarn.

Rnd1: make 66 ch, sl st in first st. (66 ch)

Rnd2: ch 1 (never count as stitch), 1dc in each st across the row, sl st in first st. (66 dc)

Rnd3: ch1, make 1 fpdc in 1st st, 1bpdc in 2nd st. Repeat the sequence. Sl st in first st. (66 sts)

Rnd4-5: repeat rnd 3. (66 sts)

Rnd6: (with peach color) ch1, 16sc, 3ch, 33sc, 3ch,17sc. Sl st in first st. (60 sc)

Rnd7: (with blue color) ch2, *3dc in 3sts, ch1, skip 1 st* repeat until reach 3ch space of previous row. Make *3dc, ch3, 3dc* in ch3 space. ch1, skip 1 ch, *3dc in 3sts, ch1, skip 1 st* repeat until next 3ch space. Make *3dc, ch3, 3dc* in ch3 space. *3dc in 3sts, ch1, skip 1 st* until last st. Slst in last st. (60 dc)

Rnd8: ch2, make *3dc, ch1* in each of ch 1 space, make *3dc, ch2, 3dc* in both ch 3 spaces.

Rnd9-: repeat rnd 8.

Rnd10-12: (with peach color) repeat rnd 8.

Rnd13-15: (with blue color) repeat rnd 8.

Rnd16-17: (with peach color) repeat rnd 8.

Rnd18-19: (with blue color) repeat rnd 8.

Edging: make 1sc in ch1 space, 9dc in next ch1 space, repeat across the row. Slst in first st. Cut the yarn and weave in ends.

Crochet Gloves Pattern

Size – this gloves pattern is in 3 sizes. You can increase finger portion length by adding more lines in the end.

Materials:

- Yarn – Alize cotton yarn in peach color (or any color of your choice)
- Hook– 4.5mm crochet hooks
- Tapestry needle, scissors
- Stitches used – chain (ch), double crochet (dc), frontpost double crochet (fpdc), backpost double crochet (bpdc), slip stitch (sl st), st (stitch), [..] total number of stitches

Directions:

Rnd1: make 26,30,34 ch, sl st in first st. (26,30,34 ch)

Rnd2: ch 1 (never count as stitch), 1dc in each st across the row, sl st in first st. (26,30,34 dc)

Rnd3: ch1, make 1 fpdc in 1st st, 1bpdc in 2nd st. Repeat the sequence. Sl st in first st. (26,30,34 sts)

Rnd4: repeat rnd 3. (26,30,34 sts)

Rnd5: ch1, make 5 dc, 3dc in next st, 1dc in each st across the row. sl st in first st. (28,32,36 sc)

Rnd6: ch1, make 5 dc, 2dc in next st, 1dc in next st, 2dc in next st, 1dc in each st across the row. sl st in first st. (30,34,38 sc)

Rnd7: ch1, make 5 dc, 2dc in next st, 3dc in next 3 st, 2dc in next st, 1dc in each st across the row. sl st in first st. (32,36,40 sc)

Rnd8: ch1, make 5 dc, 2dc in next st, 5dc in next 5 st, 2dc in next st, 1dc in each st across the row. sl st in first st. (34,38,44 sc)

Rnd9: ch1, 6dc, ch1, skip next 7 sts, 1dc in each st across the row. sl st in first st. (27,31,35 dc)

Rnd10-13: ch1, 1dc in each st across the row. sl st in first st. (28,32,36 dc)

Cut the yarn and weave in ends.

Ugg Boots for Newborn

Size – newborn

Materials:

- Yarn – Alize cotton yarn in blue color, a piece of white yarn
- Hook– 4.5mm crochet hooks
- Tapestry needle, scissors
- Stitches used – chain (ch), single crochet (sc), half double crochet (hdc), double crochet (dc), double crochet decrease (dcd), slip stitch (sl st), st (stitch), [..] total number of stitches

Directions:

Rnd1: make 12 ch. (12ch)

Rnd2: count 2 ch as 1st dc, 2dc in 3rd ch from hook, 8dc in next 8 ch, 5dc in last ch, 8dc on other side, 2dc in the last ch (total 5 dc including ch2). sl st in first st. (26 dc)

Rnd3: ch1 (don't count as stitch), 2dc in each next 3 st, 8dc in next 8st, 2dc in each next 5 st, 8dc in next 8st, 2dc in each next 2 st. sl st in first dc. (36 sts)

Rnd4: ch1, 1dc in each st across the row. (36 sts)

Rnd5: ch1, 12sc in next 12 sts, 1hdc, 5dcd, 1hdc, 12sc in next 12 sts. sl st in first st. (31 sts)

Rnd6: ch1, 10sc in next 10 sts, 1hdc, 2dcd, 1dc, 2dcd, 1hdc, 10sc in next 10 sts. sl st in first st. (27 sts)

Rnd7: ch1, 10sc, 1hdc, 1dcd, 1dc, 1dcd, 1hdc, 10 sc. sl st in first st. (25 sts)

Rnd8-10: 1dc in each st across the row. sl st in first st. (25 dc)

Rnd11: 1sc in each st across the row. sl st in first st. (25 sts)

Cut the yarn and weave in ends.

Use white yarn to make laces.

Crochet Scarf Pattern

Materials:

- Yarn – Alize cotton yarn in maroon

- Hook– 4.5mm crochet hooks

- Tapestry needle, scissors

- Stitches used – chain (ch), single crochet (sc), double crochet (dc), st (stitch), [..] total number of stitches

Directions:

Start with 50 ch.

Rnd 1: skip 1 ch, 49 sc. (49 sc)

Rnd 2: ch2 (count as 1 dc) , *skip 2 sts, make (3dc, 3ch, 3dc) in same st, skip 2 sts, 1dc in next st* repeat from * to * across the row. (49 dc)

Rnd 3: ch2, *make (3dc, 3ch, 3dc) in ch 3 space, 1dc in next st* repeat across the row. (49 dc)

Rnd 4-82: repeat rnd 3.

Rnd 83: *1sc in 4 sts, 1sc in ch1 sp* repeat across the rnd. (57 sc)

110

Crochet Earrings pattern

Materials:

- Yarn – Alize cotton yarn in yellow (or any color of your choice)

- Hook– 2mm crochet hooks

- Tapestry needle, scissors, hanging beads, earring materials

- Stitches used – chain (ch), single crochet (sc), double crochet (dc), double crochet decrease (dcd), st (stitch), [..] total number of stitches

Directions:

Start with 10 ch. Slst in 1st ch to form a ring.

Rnd 1: ch2 (count as 1st dc), 23 dc in the ring. (24 dc)

Rnd 2: make *1dcd, ch3, skip 2sts* x 8. (8 dcd)

Rnd 3: *1sc, 7dc, 1sc in each ch 3 space* x 8. (72 sts)

Cut the yarn and weave in ends. Join with earrings. Attach a hanging bead.

Baby Belly Shoes

Materials:

- Yarn – Alize cotton yarn in off white, pink and green color
- Hook– 4.5mm crochet hooks

118

- Tapestry needle, scissors
- Stitches used – chain (ch), single crochet (sc), half double crochet (hdc), double crochet (dc), double crochet decrease (dcd), st (stitch), [..] total number of stitches

Directions:

Start with ch 15.

Rnd 1: skip 2 ch(count as 1st dc), 2dc in 3rd ch, 11 dc, 5dc in last ch, turn, 11 dc on other side of the ch, 2dc in 1st ch. slst. (32 dc)

Rnd 2: *2dc in each st* x 3, 11 dc, *2dc* x 5*, 11 dc, *2dc* x 2. (42 dc)

Rnd 3: ch1 (don't count as stitch), 17 hdc, 5dcd, 15 hdc. Slst. (37 sts)

Rnd 4: ch1, 15hdc, 2dcd, 1dc, 2dcd, 13 hdc. slst. (33 sts)

Rnd 5: ch1, 13 hdc, 2dcd, 1dc, 2dcd, 11 hdc. Slst. (29 sts)

Flower:

Rnd 1: ch 56

Rnd 2: skip 1 ch, *1sc, skip next 2 sts, 5dc in same st, skip 2 sts* x 9. End with sc. slst.

Leave a long tail before cutting the yarn. Start folding the flower from 1 petal. After folding completely use the needle to stitch flower.

Leaves:

Rnd 1: ch 9

Rnd 2: skip 2 ch (count as 1st dc), 1 dc in 3rd ch, 5dc in next st, 2dc in next st,(one leaf is complete), 1sc, (2nd leaf) 2dc, 5dc, 2dc. slst.

Stitch flower and leaf on shoes. Make a long chain to make a shoe tie.

Crochet Rose Flower

Materials:

- Yarn – Alize cotton yarn in yellow

- Hook– 5mm crochet hooks

- Tapestry needle, scissors

- Stitches used – chain (ch), single crochet (sc), double crochet (dc), st (stitch), [..] total number of stitches

Directions:

Start with ch 58 ch

Rnd 1: skip 5ch (count as 1dc and 3ch), 1dc, *ch1, (1dc, ch3, 1dc) in same st* x 17. (72 dc)

Rnd 2: 1sc, *7dc in ch 3 space, 1sc in ch1 space* x 18. (126 dc)

Fold the flower from 1st petal to last petal. Stitch bottom part with needle.

Six Petals Flower

Materials:

- Yarn – Alize cotton yarn in peach (or any color of your choice)
- Hook– 4mm crochet hooks
- Tapestry needle, scissors, hanging beads, earring materials

- Stitches used – chain (ch), double crochet (dc), fifth crochet (fc), slip stitch (slst), st (stitch), [..] total number of stitches

*fifth crochet: yarn over 4 times, insert hook in under the chain and pull a loop. Now there are 5 loops on the hook. Yarn over and pull a loop through 2 loops, repeat this step 4 times.

Directions:

Start with magic ring

Rnd 1: make *1 dc, ch 2* x 6 in the magic ring. Slst. (6 dc)

Rnd 2: *ch3, 4dc in ch 3 space, ch3 slst in next st* x 6. (24 dc)

Rnd 3: ch1, *1sc in 1st dc of rnd 1, ch4* x 6. Slst. (6 sc)

Rnd 4: *ch5, 6 fc in ch4 space, ch5, slst in next st* x 6. (36 fc)

Cut the yarn and weave in ends.

Crochet Baby Cape

Materials:

- Yarn – Alize cotton yarn in yellow and white

- Hook– 4.5mm crochet hooks

- Tapestry needle, scissors, big black buttons

- Stitches used – chain (ch), single crochet (sc), double crochet (dc), front post double crochet (fpdc), back post double crochet (bpdc), st (stitch), [..] total number of stitches

Directions:

Panels (make 2)

Start with 33 ch.

Rnd 1: skip 1 ch, 32 sc. (32 sc)

Rnd 2: 1dc, skip 1 st, *make 3dc in same st, skip 2 sts* x 10, 1dc in last st. (32 dc)

Rnd 3-19: repeat rnd 3.

Shoulder:

Rnd 20 a: 1dc, skip 1 st, *make 3dc in same st, skip 2 sts* x 3, 1dc. (11 dc)

Rnd 21-22 b: repeat rnd 20 a.

Rnd 20 b: repeat rnd 20 a to make 2nd shoulder.

Rnd 21-22: repeat rnd 21-22 b.

Now stitch shoulders of both panels, together.

Neck:

Rnd 1: make 1dc in each st of rnd 19, make 2 dc in st of rnd 20-22. Slst to form a ring. (44 dc)

Rnd 2: make *1fpdc, 1bpdc* x 22. Slst. (44 dc)

Rnd 3-6: repeat rnd 2.

Make a border of front post and back post crochet on all sides. Attach buttons on both sides.

Neck Cowl Pattern

Size – adult

Materials:

- Yarn – Alize cotton yarn in beige color
- Hook– 4.5mm crochet hooks
- Tapestry needle, scissors
- Black buttons
- Stitches used – chain (ch), single crochet (sc)

Directions:

Row1: make 151 ch. (151ch)

Row2: 1sc in 2nd ch form hook. 1sc in each st across the row. (150 sc)

Row3-: ch1 (don't count as stitch), 1sc in front loop only. Repeat across the row. (150 sc)

Row4-22: repeat row 3. (150 sc)

Cut the yarn and weave in ends. Stitch buttons.

Floral Jewelry Pattern

Materials:

- Yarn – size 14 thread or parachute thread in white color (or any color of your choice)
- Hook– 1.5mm crochet hooks
- needle, scissors
- Transparent round beads in large and small sizes, chain, earring loops.
- Pliers, glue for stiffening
- Stitches used – chain (ch), treble crochet (tr), slip stitch (sl st)

Directions:

Work in magic ring.

Rnd1: make 3 ch, 5tr, 3 ch, sl st in the ring. This is one petal now make 4 more petals.

Cut the yarn and weave in ends.

Make 5 flowers. 2 flowers are for ear studs and 3 for the necklace. Mix water and glue in a 1:1 ratio and apply on the backside of flowers with a brush. Wait for drying. Assemble all things together.

Sheep Plushie

Materials:

- Yarn – Alize cotton gold yarn (or DMC natura) for legs, ears, muzzle, and tail / yarn art dolce (or Sirdar Smudge yarn) for head and body

- Hook–2MM and 3.5mm crochet hooks

- Stitches used – single crochet (sc), slip stitch (sl st), st (stitch), [..] total number of stitches Tapestry needle, scissors, stuffing

- 2 felt circles of white color, which is optional, and 2 black beads or half beads for eyes

- Black embroidery yarn

Directions:

Stuff the parts as you go (except the ears).

HEAD:

Start with Alize cotton gold; take2.0mm crochet hook.

Rnd1:6 sc in a magic ring

Rnd2: (inc) repeat 6 times

Rnd3: (sc in the next st, inc) repeat 6 times

Rnd4: (sc in the next 2st, inc) repeat 6 times

Rnd5: (sc in the next 3st, inc) repeat 6 times

Rnd6: (sc in the next 4 st, inc) repeat 6 times

Rnd7-12: sc in all 36 st.

Rnd13: (sc in the next 4 st, dec) repeat 6 times

Rnd14: sc in all 30st.

Rnd15: (sc in the next 3 st, dec) repeat 6 times

Change yarn to Yarn Art Do lce and take 3.5mm crochet hook.

Rnd16-19: sc in all 24st.

Rnd20: (sc in the next 2st, dec) repeat 6 times

Rnd21: (sc in the next st, dec) repeat 6 times

Rnd22: (dec) repeat 6times

Fasten off, hide the ends.

EAR (make 2)

With Alize cotton Gold and 2MM crochet hook.

Rnd1: sc in a magic ring.

Rnd2: (inc) repeat 6 times

Rnd3-9: sc in all 12 st.

Fasten off, leaving a tail for sewing.

BODY

WithYarn Art dolce yarn and 3.5mm crochet hook

Rnd1:6 sc in a magic ring

Rnd2: (inc) repeat 6 times

Rnd3: (sc in the next st, inc) repeat 6 times

Rnd4: (sc in the next 2st,inc) repeat 6 times

Rnd5: (sc in the next 3st, inc) repeat 6 times

Rnd6: (sc in the next 4 st, inc) repeat 6 times

Rnd7-10: sc in all 36 st.

Rnd11: (sc in the next 4 st, dec) repeat 6 times

Rnd12: sc in all 30st.

Rnd13: (sc in the next 2st, dec) repeat 6 times

Rnd 14: Sc in all 18st.

Rnd15: (sc in the next st, dec) repeat 6 times

Rnd16: (dec) repeat 6times

Fasten off, hide the ends.

LEGS (make 2)

With Alize cotton gold and 2MM crochet hook

Rnd1: 6sc in a magic ring.

Rnd2: (inc) repeat 6 times

Rnd3: (sc in the next st, inc) repeat 6 times

Rnd4-6: sc in all 18st.

Rnd7: (dec, sc in the next 7st) repeat 2 times

Rnd8: (dec, sc in the next 6 st) repeat 2 times

Rnd9: (dec, sc in the next 5 st) repeat 2 times

Rnd10: (dec, sc in the next 4 st) repeat 2 times

Rnd11: (dec, sc in the next 3 st) repeat 2 times[8]

Rnd12-27: sc in all 8 st.

Fasten off, leaving a tail for sewing. Do not stuff firmly, just a little bit and enough to fill.

ARMS

With Alize cotton gold and 2MM crochet hook

Rnd 1: 6 sc in a magic ring.

Rnd 2: (inc) repeat 6 times

Rnd 3-6: sc in all 12 st.

Rnd 7: (dec, sc in the next 4 st) repeat 2 times

Rnd 8: (dec, sc in the next 3 st) repeat 2 times [8]

Rnd 9-22: sc in all 8 st.

Fasten off, leaving a tail for sewing. Do not stuff firmly, just a little bit and enough to fill.

TAIL

With Alize cotton gold and 2MM crochet hook.

Rnd 1: 6 sc in a magic ring

Rnd 2: (inc) repeat 6 times

Rnd 3: (sc in the next 1 st, dec) repeat until the end of the round [6] Fasten off, leaving a tail for sewing.

Assemble all the parts, attach the eye, then embroider the muzzle. Your sheep amigurumi is now completed!

Crochet Doll

Materials:

- Yarn – Approximately 150G size 4 yarn Hook
  Size 3.75 - 3.5 mm hook

- Stitches used– single crochet (sc), single crochet
  increase (2 sc in each stitch), invisible decrease
  (inv dec), magic circle

- Tapestry needle, scissors, stuffing

  10.5mm safety eyes

- Yarn for hair and

  clothes stitch marker

Directions:

1. To do an invisible decrease, put the hook through the front loop only of two consecutive stitches (two loops on hook). Yarn over pull through both loops [two loops on hook]. Yarn over pull through two loops.

2. To make a magic circle, make a loop, leaving a long tail to work with. Insert hook in the center of loop, yarn over, and draw up a loop. Yarn over, pull through to make the first chain (this does not count as a stitch). Continue to crochet over the loop and tail with the number of stitches called for. For example, if you need 5sc, then crochet 5sc inside the ring. Pull the tail to close the circle. Always move your stitch marker to the last stitch in the round. This pattern is worked in a continuous round. Lightly stuff as yougo.

LEGS(use   slipper   color)

Round1: In a magic circle, sc 6 .

Round2: sc inc in each stitch around. (12)

Round3: sc in first, sc inc in next. Repeat around.(18)

Round4-10: sc in each stitch around (18)

Change to skin color.

Rounds11-38: sc in each stitch around (18) Fasten

off.

Repeat for the second leg but do not fasten off. Instead, chain 3 and then sc in the next stitch of the other leg. Keep in mind to crochet the tail left over by fastening off. Sc around the entire leg. When you come to the three chains, sc in each chain around the next leg. Sc over the chain back to the other leg. In the last sc on the last chain, place your chain marker. This is your round39.

Rou nd 40: sc around (2)

If you are making a dress, you can change the yarn to match the dress color of your choice at this point.

Round41-60: sc around (42)

At this point, change back to skin color. Crochet in the back loop only for the first row of skin color. While this is optional, it is a good consideration because it provides cleaner lines.

Round61:4 sc, inv dec, repeat around. (35)

Round62: 3sc, inv dec, repeat around. (28)

Round63: 2sc, inv dec, repeat around. (21)

Round64: 1sc, inv dec, repeat around. (14) **Round65:** 4

sc, sc in each stitch around. (14)

Inc dec until you have 12 stitches on the round. From this point, you will be increasing the head. Reset the number on the rounds.

Round66: of the body is now round 1 of the head. This way, it will be easy to check for eye/mask placement and overall general counting.

HEAD

Round1: sc in first, sc inc in next. Repeat around. (18)

Round2: sc in first 2, sc inc in next. Repeat around. (24)

Round3:sc in first 3, sc inc in next. Repeat around. (30) **Round4:** sc

in first 4, sc inc in next. Repeat around. (36) **Round5:** sc in first 5, sc

inc in next. Repeat around. (42) **Round6:** sc in first 6, sc inc in next.

Repeat around. (48) **Round7:** sc in first 7, sc inc in next. Repeat

around. (54) **Round8-23:** sc in each stitch around. (54)

Put the safety eyes in between rows 15 and 16, about 9 stitches apart. Make sure they fit well by lining up your mask. Sew the eye lashes at this point. This is also a good time to place the foam roller or dowel if you are using one. Make sure to stuff the neck around the dowel as well as you can.

Round24: sc in first 7, inv dec in next. Repeat around. (48) **Round25:** sc

in first 6, inv dec in next. Repeat around.(42) **Round26:** sc in first 5,inv

dec in next. Repeat around. (36) **Round27:** sc in first 4, inv dec in next.

Repeat around. (30) **Round28:** sc in first 3, inv dec in next. Repeat

around. (24) **Round29:** sc in first 2, inv dec in next. Repeat around. (18)

Round 30: sc in the first, inv dec in next. Repeat around. (12)

Round 31: inv dec around. (6)

Fasten off and carefully sew the remaining hole closed. Leave a long tail to make a nose.

ARMS

Round 1: In a magic circle, sc 6. (6)

Round 2: inc in each around. (12)

Rounds 3-28: sc in each stitch around. (12)

Stuff lightly and attach it to the body. Sew these on between rows 62 and 63.

If you are adding sleeves, only go to row 23 with the skin color. Change to the dress color and finish the 5 remaining rows.

HAIR

First, make the hair hat. This is not worked into the round, as you will attach this with a slip stitch to the first stitch after each row. Use a larger hook such as 4.5mm size hook.

Row 1: dc 10 in a magic circle.

Row 2: dc inc in each around.

Row 3: dc in the first, dc inc in the next. Repeat around.

Row 4: dc in the first 2, dc in the next. Repeat around.

Row 5-8: dc in each around.

Fasten off and leave a long tail for sewing into the head.

Simple Slouch Beanie

Materials

Medium weight yarn Crochet hook 5 mm Crochet hook 4 mm Tapestry needle Gauge

14 Double crochets x 9 rows = 4 inches

Directions

Start off the hat by making a magic loop.

Row 1: Chain 2 (this will count as the first double crochet) and then make 11 double crochets into the ring. Join to the top of chain 2 and pull loop tight (you will have 12 stitches).

Row 2: Chain 2 (this will count as the first double crochet), double crochet into the same stitch,

*2 double crochets into the next stitch*all the way round and join (you will now have 24 stitches).

Row 3: Chain 2 (this will count as the first double crochet), double crochet into the next stitch, 2 double crochets in next stitch, *double crochet into the next 2 stitches, 2 double crochets into the next stitch*. Repeat from * all the way round and join (you will now have 32 stitches).

Row 4: Chain 2 (this will count as the first double crochet), 2 double crochets into the next stitch, *double crochet into the next 3 stitches, 2 double crochets into the next stitch*. Repeat from * all the way round and join. (You will now have 40 stitches).

Row 5: Chain 2 (this will count as the first double crochet), 2 double crochets into the next stitch, *double crochet into the next 4 stitches, 2 double crochets into the next stitch*. Repeat from * all the way round and join. (You will now have 48 stitches).

Row 6: Chain 2 (this will count as the first double crochet), 2 double crochets into the next stitch, *double crochet into the next 5 stitches, 2 double crochets into the next stitch*. Repeat from * all the way round and join. (You will now have 56 stitches).

Row 7: Chain 2 (this will count as the first double crochet), 2 double crochets into the next stitch, *double crochet into the next 6 stitches, 2 double crochets into the next stitch*. Repeat from * all the way round and join. (You will now have 64 stitches).

Row 8: Chain 2 (this will count as the first double crochet), 2 double crochets into the next stitch, *double crochet into the next 7 stitches, 2 double crochets into the next stitch*. Repeat from * all the way round and join. (You will now have 72 stitches).

Row 9: Chain 2, *double crochet in each stitch*. Repeat from * all the way around and join.

Rows 10-28: Repeat the pattern in Row 9 and join. Note: Depending on how long you would like the slouch to be or the tension gauge, you will be able to add on or reduce the number of rows crochet.

Row 29: Switch to the smaller hook. Chain 1, *in back loop only, single crochet in each stitch.

*   Repeat from * all the way round and join.

Rows 30-34: Repeat the pattern in Row 29. Fasten off the yarn and weave in the loose ends.

Chapter 17: Where to Sell Your Crochet to Earn Good Money

There are many places to sell your crochet; choosing the right selling outlet depends on what you want to sell. Some crocheters prefer to sell one-off items instead of offering several different items. Others prefer to set up an online store and sell many items.

Craft Fairs & Shows

Craft fairs and craft shows are a great place to sell your crochet items. This type of outlet is a great choice if you have enough stock to set up a stand. Crocheters who sell at fairs and shows usually have several different items to offer; they spend the off-season crocheting their stock and getting ready for show season. If you want to sell your items but don't want to manage a store, selling at fairs and shows maybe for you. Do a little research in your area to find the fairs and shows that are close to your area. Churches, schools, local clubs, fire stations, and community centers are a few of the organizations that hold craft fairs and shows.

Once you find the fairs and shows you are interested in attending, you pay for a table/stall/stand in the fair or show. Once you pay, you are guaranteed a space, and you will be informed of how much room you will have, or how many tables.

Somes hows provide tables, others make you bring your own, the organization holding the fair or show will provide you with all the information you will need.

Set your prices according to the time you spent making your items, and include the materials you used. Search online to get an idea of what others are charging for the same type of items; this will help you set your prices and keep you competitive. You can even go to a few fairs and shows to check out the competition before you join in.

You can make your own tags for your items and include the price. There are many sites on the Internet where you can create your own tags and print them out. If you are extra crafty, you can create your own with stamps, inks, or any other media you want.

After you have tagged your items, choose a representative from each item you are selling, and display it at your stand so customers can see the merchandise. The rest of your stock should be kept bagged to stay clean and fresh during setup and transit. There are many different sized plastic bags you can use, you can find these bags at craft stores, online, or in your local super market. Bag every item you make and make sure your tags are clearly visible.

You can use your crafting skills to make your stand eye-catching and bring in customers. Use your display items to decorate your space, use a quilt stand to display afghans or baby blankets, and create a sign for yourself. If you plan to go to more than one fair or show, create a name for yourself and your merchandise, so customers will remember where they got that awesome crochet headband! Make business cards for your stand too, and be sure to place one in every bag.

Here is a list of top-selling crochet items at craft fairs and shows:

- Crochet headbands & ear warmers

- Crochet cowls and scarves

- Baby items

- Boot cuffs

- Pot holders

- Dish towels and dish cloths

- Shawls

- Slippers and socks

- Character hats

This list is not the be-all-end-all of selling at shows and fairs, but these items sell quickly and will give you a decent profit margin. If you have created a pattern for something unique, this is the place to sell it! Those who frequent craft fairs and shows are always on the lookout for unique items they haven't seen before.

Online Market Places

Amazon, Etsy, and eBay are three of the most popular online market places. Using an online marketplace to sell your crochet items is easy, time-saving, and cost-effective. One of the best things about selling on one of these sites is seeing what others are charging and what items are selling the best. A simple search for the top sellers in "crochet" will give you an idea of what to sell and what to charge. EBay uses a seller reputation system to provide consumers with feedback about the seller they plan to buy from. Your reputation on eBay is important if you want to establish a customer base; the better your reputation, the more customers will trust you, and the more money you will make.

On eBay you will need a seller name, and you will have the option to fill out a page about yourself and your items. This is where you begin to establish your reputation. Fill out these pages to give consumers an idea of who they are dealing with; this builds trust. Express your passion for crochet, let potential customers know you love what you do and that you are knowledgeable about the items you sell. When you do sell an item, always leave feedback, this will prompt your customers to do the same.

When selling on eBay, always use pictures of your items. Learn how to take the best pictures you can; it is possible to take excellent pictures with your smart phone. Check out some "how to" sites on the Internet on how to take product pictures. Many sites will walk you through everything you need to know, from lighting to editing. Remember, the better the picture, the easier it is to sell.

eBay is an auction site; it gives you the option to sell to the highest bidder or set a "buy now" option. Many people like to bid, and just as many prefer to buy it now. Choose whichever you are comfortable with. Bidding takes longer to sell an item because consumers are given time to bid against each other. The buy it now option is just what it says, buy it now.

If you decide to sell on eBay, you will need to create some selling policies, and these will be listed with your item. You will need to clearly state your return policy or no returns and give a time limit.

When you setup your seller profile, you will choose payment methods to accept. PayPal is one payment plate from accepted all over the Internet. PayPal makes it easy to accept all types of payments from customers. You will also have to choose shipping methods; eBay explains all about shipping, seller policies, and payment types when you signup.

Amazon is similar to eBay, but they have different policies and rules for sellers to adhere to. These will help you gain trust with consumers and make selling your items easier. Rules for selling on Amazon and similar sites change from time to time, so it is best to go to the site and read through their rules and guidelines.

Again, any market place site you choose to sell on will require pictures of your items, seller policies for returns and refunds (some sites require you to adhere to their return and refund policies), shipping methods (the site will guide you through this), payment methods, and seller profiles (most sites have this feature).

Items that are popular in marketplace sites change from time to time. Always search for "top sellers" or "best sellers," this will give you an idea of what is selling and how much it is selling for. When you sell at an online market place, you will be charged a fee; this varies depending on the site, it is usually a percentage of your item price, and some will charge an upfront flat fee.

Open Your Own Online Store

If you are a prolific crocheter and have enough items to sell, opening your own online store may be the best choice for you. If you open your own store, you set the rules and policies. Opening it is actually easy and cost-effective. Running an online store is similar to a brick and mortar business, but the overhead is way cheaper, and you don't have to hire employees!

There are many e-Commerce building businesses that specialize in creating websites for stores. Some companies offer the tools to build your own site and then charge a monthly fee. These companies have different skills they offer for a fee; some will even generate customers for your web store!

Here is a list of web sites that offer web hosting/building and marketing:

- Shopify

- Volusion

- Square Space

- Wix

- 3Dcart

There are many more e-Commerce builders; the main difference is in what they offer and how much the charge. Most of them charge monthly for the online store; prices vary, but they all have affordable options. Some even have tools for tracking your sales, projecting profits, and other   e-Commerce tools.

This is a list of things you will need when you decide to open an online store

- A logo (something customers will remember, important for marketing)

- Stock (this is always a good idea when you open a store!)

- A marketing plan

- An easy to use and maintain online store front/store

- Well defined and clearly stated store policies

- Pictures of your products

Another excellent idea for your store is a blog. Customers today love to read blogs about the items they are interested in purchasing. If you don't write, it is worth finding a writer to do this for you.

A "crochet" blog will help you generate sales and keep customers coming back. Use the blog to introduce your products, your passion, and throw in a few free crochet patterns; cover topics that are interesting to you as a crochet artist, and they will be interesting to those who buy crochet items.

Conclusion

Learning to crochet is a skill you will find useful because you can take what you know and turn it into garments and projects that provide joy and utility for people who use them. There is a large variety of uses for the crochet stitches covered in this book. With your imagination, you can take your new knowledge of the stitches and create your own patterns and designs to make a variety of projects of your own.

Keep your hands relaxed so that you are not tensing up and tiring your fingers and hands. By relaxing, your stitches will come freely, and by practicing, you will be able to unravel the stitches that don't measure up to your standard, retry the stitches over and over again. You will find you like some stitches more than others. By mastering the basic stitches, you will be able to tolerate your least favorites. The first row is always the most grueling. Make sure your foundation chain is even and not too tight. This will make it easier to fit the hook into the chain when you are making the first row of stitches. It will come easier as time goes by and you practice more.

Take the stitches you have learned and makes watches of the stitches. This practice will pay off handsomely as you perfect the stitches and grow comfortable handling crochet hooks of different sizes. Practicing is the best way to feel good about your skills. You will be able to see how much easier the stitches are made when you are familiar with how the yarn feels in your hands and how it moves along the crochet hook. This book takes away the intimidating features of crochet. The language of crochet is defined, and the patterns are explained in plain English. Join the crochet community by putting your new skills into action. Do the projects in the book and you'll see why people enjoy crochet and all that it has to offer. Relax and enjoy using what you learn to produce actual items that you can use and enjoy.

Before you start knitting, you have to consider a series of tips that will make your life as a weaver much easier than you think. As you go above the needles and find a position that is comfortable for you to wear the strand when knitting, you will gradually relax, let go of the knitting, and find your own "tension of weaver."

When you start knitting, it is often above whelming that the wool escapes between your fingers, the needles are drained, and the stitches are released while knitting. This insecurity that causes us to face something new makes us weave the point very tightly. It's totally normal for this to happen, and you don't have to get overwhelmed or give it a lot of importance. You're not going to weave that tight always.

But until that happens, it is advisable to start knitting with the right needles. So, what are the right needles when you start knitting? The first thing you should know is that there are no good needles or bad needles in themselves. In principle, each type of needle is designed for a type of fiber and a type of weaver.

CPSIA information can be obtained
at www.ICGtesting.com
Printed in the USA
BVHW060627070521
606649BV00005B/1056